AI FOR IMMUNOLOGY

AI FOR EVERYTHING

Artificial intelligence (AI) is all around us. From driverless cars to game winning computers to fraud protection, AI is already involved in many aspects of life, and its impact will only continue to grow in future. Many of the world's most valuable companies are investing heavily in AI research and development, and not a day goes by without news of cutting-edge breakthroughs in AI and robotics.

The AI for Everything series will explore the role of AI in contemporary life, from cars and aircraft to medicine, education, fashion and beyond. Concise and accessible, each book is written by an expert in the field and will bring the study and reality of AI to a broad readership including interested professionals, students, researchers, and lay readers.

AI for Immunology
Louis J. Catania

AI for Cars
Hanky Sjafrie & Josep Aulinas

AI for Fashion
Anthony Brew, Ralf Herbrich,
Christopher Gandrud, Roland Vollgraf,
Reza Shirvany & Ana Peleteiro Ramallo

AI for Death and Dying
Maggi Savin-Baden

AI for Radiology
Oge Marques

AI for Games
Ian Millington

AI for School Teachers
Rose Luckin & Karine George

AI for Learners
Carmel Kent, Benedict du Boulay &
Rose Luckin

AI for Social Justice
Alan Dix and Clara Crivellaro

For more information about this series please visit:
https://www.routledge.com/AI-for-Everything/book-series/AIFE

AI FOR IMMUNOLOGY

LOUIS J. CATANIA, O.D., F.A.A.O., D.SC. (HON)

Senior Clinical Associate, Nicolitz
Eye Consultants

Visiting Professor, Salus University,
College of Health Sciences

Instructor, University of North
Florida, Division of Continuing
Education

CRC Press
Taylor & Francis Group
Boca Raton London New York

CRC Press is an imprint of the
Taylor & Francis Group, an informa business

First Edition published 2021
by CRC Press
2 Park Square, Milton Park, Abingdon, Oxon, OX14 4RN

and by CRC Press
6000 Broken Sound Parkway NW, Suite 300, Boca Raton, FL 33487-2742

CRC Press is an imprint of Informa UK Limited

British Library Cataloguing-in-Publication Data
A catalogue record for this book is available from the British Library

ISBN: 978-0-367-68521-8 (hbk)
ISBN: 978-0-367-65465-8 (pbk)
ISBN: 978-1-003-13793-1 (ebk)

Typeset in Joanna
by codeMantra

eResources are available at www.routledge.com/9780367654658

To Russell
I'll always remember.

To all the health care workers
who have served us all during the
COVID-19 pandemic and every day,
thank you.

To the families of all those lost
to the COVID-19 pandemic,
my deepest sympathies.

CONTENTS

PREFACE

You are about to take a deep dive into a group of five subjects, all relatively complex. Even more challenging is the fact that all five subjects are intimately related, disruptive (as in promoting change), and deeply personal (all have, and will continue to have direct and profound effects on you and your loved ones). Foreboding as this alert might seem, its promise includes an educational journey I think (I hope!) you will enjoy.

The five subjects include: (1) immunology as a bioscience; (2) chronic inflammation, an adjunct of immunology and itself, a distinct clinical entity; (3) autoimmunity, again a component of immunology, but a clinical science unto itself; (4) immunology's greatest challenge in the 21st century, the novel coronavirus (SARS-CoV-2) and the COVID-19 pandemic; and finally (5) the nexus of all four of these clinical and scientific subjects, the technology of artificial intelligence (AI), and the disruptive computer science that directly affects, soon to be, all aspects of human existence.

The timing of the writing of this book (late 2020) is providential in relationship to the epical COVID-19 pandemic the world is facing. Notwithstanding the classification of the novel coronavirus (SARS-CoV-2) as an infectious disease, its pathogenesis, clinical manifestations, and eventual vanquishing or control fall directly within the domain of our immunology subjects and their related clinical adjuncts. And given the devastating, universal nature of an infectious pandemic, another thread throughout the discussion of the subjects in this book will be AI's role in the public health implications of each science.

The challenge of addressing the multiple facets of health care, bioscience, and the significant AI applications in these categories to an audience of readers ranging from health providers, to AI (and IT) professionals, and to interested laypersons will require an organized and understandable approach. Such an approach will necessitate a brief explanation of the biological and clinical elements of these medical and biosciences followed by the relevant current and evolving AI applications, research, and their public health implications. I will tackle this challenge with major subdivisions (headings) for each science followed by a review of five related AI applications for each. In addition, AI research and future applications related to general immunology will also be addressed in a closing chapter.

Please understand that certain portions of the text might be developed at a more basic level than you feel necessary. This is being done to help educate the reader with less or no appreciable background in AI, medical, or the bioscience fields. No discussion at any level is intended to be patronizing or condescending, as I hope no one will interpret it as such.

If you find the subject of immunology interesting and find the simple graphics approach I use in Chapters 2 and 3 of this book valuable, its primary source is a book chapter I wrote 25 years ago (see Endnote #1 and in Chapter 2). The book is on eye care ("my previous life"), but I had already started studying and working in immunology back then and decided to add a comprehensive chapter (60 pages in narrative outline form) from which I extracted a limited amount of information and updates for Chapters 2 and 3 of this book. In doing the research for this current book, I was surprised at how well the information and theories I had proposed back in 1996 have held up and have been reaffirmed over time. This is not meant as a "backdoor plug" for this 1996 book. Actually, it is out of print. But if you might want an expanded, fully illustrated version of the immunology information I present in Chapters 2 and 3, CRC/Taylor and Francis (publisher of this book) has made it available on their website (https://www.routledge.com/9780367685218) as a PDF download at no charge. Of course, there are many great sources for additional reading on immunology, but I genuinely feel the step-by-step, graphic approach I use is an understandable, "user-friendly" version of an otherwise complex subject.[1]

Immunology is the fundamental science that dictates our health and well-being. It is a subject of which we should all have a working knowledge. AI's role in the science is making it infinitely more important, more influential, and more valuable to humanity. This may be a short book, but it may well be one of the most valuable ones you'll read in the interest of your and your loved ones' health and wellness. It is one from which you will be able to capture the essence of immunology, the body's system that paradoxically functions as "our best friend" and "our worst enemy." And with the help of AI, it is also the system that will address and hopefully defeat the novel coronavirus and COVID-19, protect your health, and strengthen and enhance our public health.

A full Glossary of Abbreviations and Terminology used in this book is available as a downloadable eResource at https://www.routledge.com/9780367685218

There is critically valuable information in the pages ahead. Please read on and I hope you enjoy the journey.

NOTE

1 Catania LJ. *Primary care of the anterior segment 2nd edition (textbook)*. New York: McGraw-Hill. Chapter 2. Clinical considerations on anterior segment pathology and immunology; January 1996. pp. 22–82.

ACKNOWLEDGMENTS

This book could be considered a relatively short text on a relatively complicated topic. It reminds me of the maxim quoted over the years by numerous historical figures (Abe Lincoln, Mark Twain, Woodrow Wilson, et al.) regarding speech preparation: "If you want me to speak for an hour, I am ready today. If you want me to speak for just a few minutes, it will take me a few weeks to prepare." So too is writing a short text on the complex subject of artificial intelligence (AI) and immunology, especially in this time of a foreboding pandemic. Communicating such important information coherently and concisely requires far more concentration and focus than waxing eloquently through a plethora of words. I hope I have found the balance.

Given the explosion of new information in AI, immunology and the evolution of an entirely new body of information regarding the epical COVID-19 pandemic required significant time and "concentrated energy" in research and documentation. Such an effort would be impossible without the scientific, public health, and clinical Internet search engines now available. I can assure you that this book could not have happened without the invaluable assistance of PubMed, Medline, and MedlinePlus databases provided by the U.S. National Institute of Medicine, National Institute of Health, and Center for Disease Control and Prevention, and by powerful search engines such as Google Scholar, ScienceDirect, and Scopus. As with any technical, scientific author, I must acknowledge and thank these resources for making this book a reality.

Nor could this book have happened without the professional dedication and skills of the team of CRC Press/Taylor and Francis Group editors and production staff who worked so closely with me to make this important and timely text possible. From the patience and caring of my acquisition editor, Elliott Morsia, to the production editor, Todd Perry, copyeditor, Regina, and Kritheka, and a whole array of skilled T&F professionals and support staff, I am truly grateful.

And finally, I give my deepest thanks and love to my dear wife, Stephanie, for her patience and acceptance of a sequestered author/husband. I plan on spending a whole lot of time making up for my extended mental absence from her with some serious, enjoyable, and relaxing "Stephanie time."

AUTHOR

Dr. Louis J. ("Lou") Catania, O.D., F.A.A.O., D.Sc. (Hon.), is an internationally acclaimed educator and a recognized expert in eye care, health care, AI, and disruptive technologies in bioscience. He has authored over 160 journal articles and nine textbooks including *Primary Care of the Anterior Segment* from Appleton and Lange, which received Baron's Five Star (highest) rating for medical textbooks. He is currently a Senior Clinical Associate with Nicolitz Eye Consultants, a multispecialty ophthalmology group in Jacksonville, FL. He is a lecturer with the University of North Florida, Department of Continuing Education, and a visiting Professor at Salus University, College of Health Sciences. During his 52-year clinical and academic career, he has taught and lectured extensively worldwide. Over the past 25 years, Dr. Catania has expanded his professional scope through postdoctoral studies in immunology, genetics, and artificial intelligence. He has been awarded innumerable honors including two Honorary Doctor of Science degrees; named Distinguished Faculty Scholar, State University of New York College of Optometry; inducted into the National Optometry Hall of Fame (2016); Honorary Lecturer at The Ohio State University (2017); and commencement speaker and honorary Doctor of Science degree from Salus University (2019).

AUTHOR

1

UNDERSTANDING ARTIFICIAL INTELLIGENCE (AI)

INTRODUCTION

The Merriam-Webster dictionary defines AI as "…a branch of computer science dealing with the simulation of intelligent behavior in computers; the capability of a machine to imitate intelligent human behavior."[1] Those simple words bespeak the magnitude of the science of AI. For "…a machine to imitate intelligent human behavior" is to have it effectively "mimic" the functions of the human brain or restated, in biologic terms, to mimic neuroscience. The neurological functions associated with intelligence are related to the cortical control centers, progressive neural layers, and the complex neural networking between these centers and layers. Thus, AI must simulate the structures of these cortical centers and layers and their neural network functioning.

While there are substantial differences between AI and basic computers, there also are some common denominators in their structure and function. The most relevant among them include three fundamental categories: (1) the input layer, components for entering "user data" (e.g., hardware such as keyboard, printers, audio/visual); (2) the inner (hidden) layer, a functional component for data processing (sequence of automated operations to convert user input data into computer language or "code") consisting of hardware like microprocessors (central processing unit [CPU], random access memory drive [RAM]) and software ("hidden" operating systems [OS] programming applications); and (3) the output layer consisting of the hardware devices (monitors, printers, audio/visual) to present computed results.

A MODEL FOR UNDERSTANDING ARTIFICIAL INTELLIGENCE

AI utilizes multiple hardware and software tools in its inner layer to effectively mimic the neurological functions associated with intelligence. These inner layer functions are classified into the two main categories of AI: "machine learning" and "deep learning." These two categories introduce unique aspects to the computing process that electronically reproduce the qualities of human intelligence. To accomplish this task, AI uses "algorithms," mathematical formulas to simulate the progressive layers of neuronal functions and neural networking in the human brain.

A simple way (kind of) to understand how AI works is to briefly present how the structures and functions of the human brain process information. Then we can compare that process to the structures and functions associated with the three layers of AI computing and its machine and deep learning process.

The fundamental neuroanatomical component of the brain that dictates neural functioning is called "the neuron." It is estimated that there are approximately 100 billion neurons in the human brain.2 Nerve impulses travel down axons reaching junctions called synapses where neurotransmitter chemicals are released across the synaptic cleft activating other neurons. All of this activity can be reduced to a mathematical model using linear algebra and differential calculus[3] (Figure 1.1).

The brain receives its user (input) data which it transmits through inner layer neuronal pathways in nuclei called the limbic system (analogous to a computer operating system [OS]). These nuclei act as relay stations that analyze input data and transmit it to appropriate higher cortical layers for interpretation. This vast network of 100 billion

Mathematical Model of the Neuron

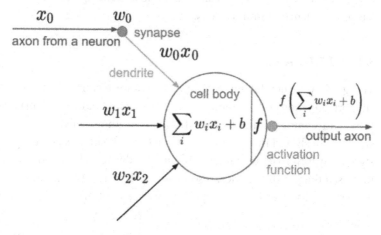

Figure 1.1 Mathematical model of neuron. (Diaa, Ahmedien [2018] The Mathematical Model of the Biological Neuron.)

interconnecting neurons creates a complex in the human brain, collectively referred to as the neural network (NN), analogous to AI algorithms. This vast network produces multilayered, convolutional interconnections called the convolutional neural network (CNN).

The CNN has the potential of producing 100 trillion neural connections.[4] This level of neural networking is called the "deep neural network" (DNN). The DNN is the analog of the AI electronic computing functions conducted by a central processing unit (CPU) and/ or a graphic processing unit (GPU); programming applications; algorithms; databases; and servers. In the human brain, the results are human intelligence (output) while the electronic computer produces AI output. The sum total of this computer process is referred to broadly as "machine learning" with the specific CNN and DNN processes called "deep learning."

These comparative analogies introduce hardware and software components associated with the science and technologies of AI.

To complete an understanding of AI, descriptions of the major software and hardware components are needed. With that understanding, you will be able to appreciate the influences and applications AI has in the science of immunology.

AI HARDWARE

The guiding principle and goal of AI hardware technology are to support the enormous volume of data processing and the calculations and computations the AI software algorithms must execute simultaneously and in milliseconds. A brief thumbnail of each of the significant forms of current and evolving hardware will provide an understanding of the physical resources that drive the AI computing process and its diverse and complex software algorithms.

RAM (RANDOM ACCESS MEMORY)

A RAM microchip is a high-speed type of computer memory device that temporarily stores all input information as well as application software instructions the computer needs immediately and in the near future. RAM is read from any layer of the computer at almost the same speed. It loses all of its dynamic memory when the computer shuts down.[5]

When thinking of RAM relative to AI computing, consider it analogous to the hippocampus nucleus of the limbic system in the neuroscience model. It uses an ANN process called "memory networking" (similar to brain "plasticity") to differentiate and adjust the connections between machine (unsupervised) and deep (supervised) learned information.[6]

CENTRAL PROCESSING UNIT (CPU)

The central processing unit (CPU) is the "brain" of the computer. It transforms the raw data into binary code (computer language) that can be manipulated and stored as memory in RAM. The CPU is the analog to the human brain at large when using our neuroscience analogy. It is the processor for all the operations the computer conducts. How your computer operates is based on mathematical operations (algorithms), and the CPU controls all of them through its arithmetic logic unit (ALU).

GRAPHIC PROCESSING UNIT (GPU)

A GPU is a specialized microprocessor optimized for displaying graphics and doing very specific computer tasks. CPUs and GPUs are both made from hundreds of millions of transistors which can process thousands of operations per second. The GPU uses thousands of smaller and more efficient cores than the CPU and can handle multiple functions of lively parallel data at the same time. GPUs are 50–100 times faster in tasks that require multiple parallel processes, such as computer graphics and gaming (for which they were initially developed by Nvidia), but its most significant value is in its iterative computations of massive data load in machine learning, deep learning, and big data analytics.[7]

SERVERS

The term "server" simply means a machine (computer) that "serves" other machines, thus the name "server machine."[8] Whereas processors and CPUs are "the brain of the computer," servers are their "heart." They are computers themselves (hardware supporting software) designed to process requests and deliver data to another computer, a local network, or over the Internet.

INTERNET OF THINGS (IoT)

A "hybrid" system known as the "Internet of Things" (IoT) is a system of interrelated computing devices, mechanical and digital machines, objects, and even people and animals that are provided with unique identifiers (UIDs) and the ability to transfer data over a network without requiring human-to-human or human-to-computer interaction.[9] All categories of industries, especially health care, are using IoTs to operate more efficiently, better understand customer and patient needs, deliver enhanced timely services, and improve decision-making and the overall efficiency of providing services.

A "thing" in the IoT can be a person with a heart monitor implant, an automobile that has built-in sensors to alert the driver when tire pressure is low, or any other natural or man-made object that can be assigned an IP address and can transfer data over a network. The next level of IoT is a sensor network of billions of smart devices (e.g., smartphones) that connects people, systems, and other applications to collect and share data.

AI SOFTWARE (ALGORITHMS)

The basic component of AI software is the algorithm. An algorithm is a procedure or formula for solving a mathematical problem based on conducting a sequence of specified actions or steps that frequently involve repetition of an operation.[10] It is the computational process using the language of mathematics. When applied in computer science, it expresses maximal, practical, efficient solutions in words to mathematical problems and questions. From the human neural network descriptions above and their potential "trillions of computations," you can begin to appreciate that in the ANN, algorithms "mimic" the human brain's functions, including those of the CNN and the DNN.

AI deals with enormous volumes of data (billions of data points) requiring incredible amounts of calculations, computations, and iterations (in the trillions) done at almost instantaneous speeds. The development of sophisticated algorithms in conjunction with the rapid development of powerful AI hardware capable of generating and delivering these incomprehensible amounts of calculations at near-instantaneous speeds is responsible for the explosion of AI computing. The frameworks within which algorithms operate are the two subcategories of AI described previously: machine learning

(ANN in our neuroscience analog) and deep learning (CNN in our neuroscience analog).

APPLICATION PROGRAMMING INTERFACE (API)

"Application programming interface," or API, is perhaps the most essential part of any computer system. It is a software intermediary (i.e., "software to software" program) whose function is to specify how software components should interact or "integrate" with databases and other programs.[11] API software algorithms interpret user input (e.g., text, data, audio, graphics, natural language processing, video, GPUs [graphic processing units], and knowledge engineers [expert systems]) to allow one computer to be used ("user input") by other computer programs (databases). Thus, APIs enable the AI computer algorithms to analyze the main factor(s) of user input ("unlabeled data") that one is attempting to understand or predict.[12]

ARTIFICIAL NEURAL NETWORK (ANN)

The two ANN frameworks, machine, and deep learning employ numerous algorithms, all utilizing complex linear algebra, multivariable and differential calculus, Bayesian logic, probabilities, and statistical mathematical calculations. This brief review of AI and its algorithms will identify those mathematical calculations used in the respective learning frameworks but will not present their specific applications. For the interested reader, detailed explanations and applications of each algorithm are available in multiple mathematical textbooks.[13,14,15]

MACHINE LEARNING

Machine learning allows computers to "learn" directly from examples and experience in the form of data. Given a large amount of data to use as examples (input) to detect patterns to determine how a task is achieved, the system learns how best to produce the desired output.[16] As with the human neural network, in machine learning, there are thousands of layers, each with thousands of nodes (points within a network), trained upon millions of data points.[17]

There are three branches of machine learning: supervised (labeled data), unsupervised (unlabeled data), and reinforcement learning. Supervised (labeled data) is usually associated with machine learning, while unsupervised (unlabeled data) and reinforcement learning refer more to deep learning.

Each branch of machine learning is driven by mathematical formulae (algorithms) that analyze data to produce answers, predictions, and insights from which the user can make decisions. A brief description of all three branches of machine and deep learning with practical examples will help to clarify their meaning.[18]

Supervised (Labeled) Data

The majority of practical machine learning uses supervised learning.[19] It is a form of learning where the user has a dataset of "labeled" input variables (x) and an output variable (y). The algorithm learns the mapping function from the input to the output by "supervising" the process. It develops "training data" from the variable's structure or pattern recognition. As it learns the correct answers, the algorithm iteratively makes predictions on the training data. The algorithm's self-modifications are called "training." The goal in supervised learning is to approximate the mapping function so well that when you have new input data (x) you can predict the output variables (y) for that data. Learning stops when the algorithm achieves an acceptable level of performance.[20]

Supervised learning problems are grouped into regression and classification problems.[21] A regression problem is when the output variable (y) is a real value, such as "dollars" or "weight." A classification problem is when the output variable (y) is a category, such as "disease" and "no disease." The process is mathematically stated as $y = f(x)$. Regression and classification analysis in supervised learning uses linear logistic; Support Vector Machine (SVM); K-Nearest Neighbors; Random Forest; polynomials; decision trees; and naïve Bayes algorithms.

DEEP LEARNING

Unsupervised (Unlabeled) Data

Unsupervised learning and semi-supervised learning (limited labeled data, but large dataset) are generally referred to as "deep learning" (CNN and DNN analogy) or a subcategory of machine learning. This process utilizes an algorithm where only input data (x) is known with no corresponding output variables (thus, "unlabeled"). The goal is to group ("cluster") the structure or distribution of the data to learn more about the data. This deep learning is called unsupervised learning because there are no correct answers. Algorithms are left to their devices to discover and present the relevant structure in the data.[22]

The computer's software interacts with specific knowledge database(s) ("unlabeled data") which includes stored data from previously labeled experiences and other preexisting, directly and indirectly related, digitally stored knowledge bases on the World Wide Web. In an AI system, information is stored by inference engine software for future deep learning experiences. The information storage allows for AI's continued and expanding learning potential similar to that of the human brain. The unsupervised learning information (active and stored) is programmed into AI software allowing the computer, using Bayesian deduction reasoning, to employ it in an active collectively, progressive analytical process that extracts synergies, improves performance(s), and continued learning.[23]

Unsupervised learning problems are grouped into clustering and association problems.[24] A clustering problem is where you want to discover the inherent groupings in the data (e.g., grouping patients by their diagnosis). An association rule learning problem is where you want to find rules that describe large portions of your data, such as people with diagnosis x also tend to have symptom y (thus, $y = f(x)$ as described previously). Association rules work based on "if/then" statements in supervised and unsupervised learning.[25] These statements help to reveal associations between independent data in a database, relational database, or other information repositories.

Algorithms used in clustering and association problems in unsupervised deep learning include K-means clustering; Hierarchical clustering; and Hidden Markov models (HMM).

Reinforcement Learning

Reinforcement learning uses rewards and punishment as signals for positive and negative results. The goal of the agent is to learn the consequences of its decisions.[26] The AI software (as with the human cortical centers) tries to maximize the most significant benefit(s) it can receive when interacting with an uncertain environment.[27] It uses a process called "memory networking," which is an artificial neural networking (ANN) using RAM to differentiate and adjust the connections between unsupervised and supervised learned information.[28]

This AI process mimics the plasticity of the human brain's limbic system and cortex. As compared to unsupervised learning, reinforcement learning is different in terms of goals. While the goal in unsupervised learning is to find similarities and differences between data points, in reinforcement learning the goal is to find a suitable action model that would maximize the total cumulative reward of the user. This form of AI learning uses Markov Decision Processes (MDPs), Q-learning, SARSA (State-Action-Reward-State-Action), Deep Q-Networks (DQN), and DDPG (Deep Deterministic Policy Gradient).

AI-RELATED COMPUTER SYSTEMS

NATURAL LANGUAGE PROCESSING (NLP)

Among the technologies of AI that make it truly more user-friendly and are having a profound effect on practical AI applications is natural language processing (NLP). NLP is a specialized software application using machine learning (ANN) and computational linguistics, enabling computers to understand and process human languages and to get computers closer to a human-level understanding of language.

Recent advances in machine learning and ANNs have allowed computers to do quite a lot of useful things with natural language processing. Deep learning (CNN) has also enabled the development of programs to perform things like language translation, semantic understanding, text summarization, and chatbots.[29]

EXPERT SYSTEMS

Perhaps, the most significant application of AI in the clinical aspects of health care delivery is the domain of "expert systems." These are AI computer programs utilizing the deep learning process to analyze stored knowledge base(s) to deduce and provide options, alternatives, suggestions, advice, etc., to health care providers through "if/then" rules, inference reasoning, and forward and backward chaining to a question, problem, or strategy. This human interface activity is communicated "provider to computer" through NLP processing and "computer to provider" through natural language generation (NLG).[30]

The "Rule-Based Expert System," the most common form of an expert system, starts with a human expert working with "knowledge engineers" to create a "knowledge database." This database stores both factual, exact information on the given subject matter as well as heuristic (trial and error, intuitive, or "rule of thumb") knowledge. The knowledge engineer then categorizes, organizes, and stores the information in the form of IF-THEN-ELSE rules to be used by the "inference engine" (an algorithm). A potentially more powerful expert system can provide knowledge in a neural network (ANN) as well. The weakness of such a deep learning approach is that the ANN is limited by its "training set" of stored knowledge ("garbage in – garbage out") and its inability to provide reasoning in an "explanation facility" or "explainable AI (XAI)."

BIG DATA ANALYTICS

Big data is an evolving term that describes a large volume of structured, semi-structured, and unstructured data that has the potential to be mined for information and used in machine learning projects and other advanced analytics applications. Big data analytics is a process of using advanced algorithms and machine learning for examining, filtering, aggregating, and modeling large datasets (big data) to discover hidden patterns, trends, conclusions, and meaningful correlations, preferences between variables to retrieve intelligent insights from the data and to drive decisions.

Big data analytics is characterized by "The 3 Vs of Big Data" of which each term describes a specific property that must be understood to capture the essence of the technology.[31]

1 Volume: How much data is there?
2 Velocity: How quickly is the data being created, moved, or accessed?
3 Variety: How many different types of sources are there?

IMMUNOINFORMATICS

The term informatics, similar to big data analytics, describes the computational science of how to use data, information, and knowledge to improve human health and the delivery of health care services.[32] Bioinformatics is thus a biological subdiscipline of informatics that is concerned with the acquisition, storage, analysis, and dissemination of biological data. And from those general disciplines flows the science of "immunoinformatic" (or computational immunology), which is the science that helps to create significant immunological information using bioinformatics software and applications.[33] Some of the main areas of immunoinformatics include vaccinology, antibody analyses, predictions regarding specific epitopes for B-cell recognition and T-cell, cancer immunotherapies, and in the field of immunogenomics.

NOTES

1 Merriam-Webster Dictionary. Merriam-Webster Inc. 2019.
2 Grafman J. A glossary of key brain science terms. *The Dana Foundation*. 2019.

3   Karpathy A. Convolutional neural networks for visual recognition. *Stanford. edu*. cs231n.github.io. 2019.

4   Zimmer C. 100 trillion connections: New efforts probe and map the brain's detailed architecture. *Scientific American*. January 2011.

5   Martindale J. What is ram? *Digital Trends*. February 3, 2019.

6   Fan S. Google's new AI gets smarter thanks to a working memory. *Singularity Hub*. November 1, 2016.

7   Alena. GPU vs. CPU computing: What to choose? *Medium*. February 8, 2018.

8   Brain M. How web servers work. *How Stuff Works*. 2019.

9   Rouse M. The internet of things (IoT). *TechTarget*. March 2019.

10   WhatIs.com. Algorithm. *TechTarget*. March 2019.

11   Beal V. API - application program interface. *Webopedia*. 2019.

12   Gallo A. A refresher on regression analysis. *Harvard Business Review*. 2015:4.

13   McElwee K. *From math to meaning: Artificial intelligence blends algorithms and applications*. Princeton, NJ: Princeton University; January 2, 2019.

14   Parbhakar A. Mathematics for AI: All the essential math topics you need. Essential list of math topics for machine learning and deep learning. *Towards Data Science*. August 9, 2018.

15   Deisenroth MP, Faisal AA, Ong CS. *Mathematics for machine learning*. Cambridge: Cambridge University Press; July 3, 2020.

16   Shalev-Shwartz S, Ben-David S. *Understanding machine learning: from theory to algorithms*. Cambridge: Cambridge University Press; 2014.

17   Paruthi A. Artificial intelligence hardware. *Medium*. December 16, 2018.

18   Ibid. 17. Paruthi.

19   Brownlee J. Supervised and unsupervised machine learning algorithms. *Machine Learning Mastery*. March 16, 2016.

20   Brownlee J. Understanding machine learning algorithms. *Machine Learning Mastery*. March 16, 2016.

21   Pereira JA, Martin H, Acher M, et al. Learning software configuration spaces: A systematic literature review. *Ground AI*. arXiv:1906.03018v1. June 7, 2019.

22   Saha S. A comprehensive guide to convolutional neural networks—the ELI5 way. *Data Science*. December 15, 2018.

23   Liang P. *Semi-supervised learning for natural language*. Cambridge: MIT Press; 2005. pp. 44–52.

24   Wen I. Data mining process in R language. *Computer Language*. October 19, 2018.

25 Sarmah H. Understanding association rule learning & its role in data mining. *Analytics India Magazine*. February 18, 2019.

26 Mayo M. 5 things to know about machine learning (18:n11). *KDnuggets*. 2018.

27 Sutton RS, Barto AG. *Reinforcement learning an introduction*. Cambridge: The MIT Press; 2012.

28 Ibid. Fan. 6.

29 Seif G. An easy introduction to natural language processing. *Data Science*. October 1, 2018.

30 ArseneIoan O, DumitracheIoana M. Expert system for medical diagnosis using software agents. *Science Direct*. doi: 10.1016/j.eswa.2014. 10.026.

31 Bresnick J. Understanding the many V's of healthcare big data analytics. *HealthITAnalytics*. June 5, 2017.

32 "What is informatics?" 2020 *American Medical Informatics Association*. Accessed April 6, 2020. https://www.amia.org/news-publications/jamia

33 Raoufi E, Hemmati M, Eftekhari S, et al. Epitope prediction by novel immunoinformatics approach: A state-of-the-art review. *Int J Pept Res Ther*. 2020;26(2):1155–1163.

2

AI AND THE BIOSCIENCE AND CLINICAL CONSIDERATIONS FOR IMMUNOLOGY

INTRODUCTION

As I mentioned in the Preface of this book (hopefully you read it), immunology can be described through the maxim, "Immunology is a battle of 'self' versus 'non-self'," and through the paradox, "Immunology is our best friend and our worst enemy." Hopefully, some simple explanations will make sense of these otherwise surreptitious statements. And more so, the discussions in the subsequent chapters in this book on the bioscience of immunology and chronic inflammation[1] and the role of artificial intelligence (AI) will give you a foundation that will help you better understand the information we are continually hearing about serious diseases, infectious pandemics and current and developing treatments and cures (e.g., immunotherapeutics, vaccines, etc.). It will also give us a better perspective on our personal health and on the public health we all seek to preserve.

One other critical element to mention at the beginning of any immunology discussion is the intimate relationship between the science of immunology and genetics, a relationship referred to as immunogenics, immunogenetics, and immunogenomics. The immune system and its activity is effectively dictated and controlled by the human genome. AI is playing an enormous role in our better understanding of this complex relationship both in health and disease. Research and advances in our understanding of the immune system and autoimmune diseases, cancers, infectious diseases, and beyond are indelibly related to immunogenetics. As such, there will be a future volume in this "AI for Everything" series addressing genetics. In this volume on "AI for Immunology," by necessity, there will be some discussion on genetics as related to immunogenetics.

INNATE (NATURAL) IMMUNITY

In this wonderful world of ours, there is "you"...and everything else. Now, think of "you" as "self" and everything else as "non-self." That "non-self" might be a substance, chemical, infectious agent (pathogen, e.g., virus), toxin (airborne, ingested, contact), and even a non-substance like mental, emotional, physiological, or physical (injury) stress, virtually anything external to "you." Your body ("self") interprets these "non-self" entities as "foreign" or the technical term, an "antigen or immunogen" (we'll stick mostly with antigen for this book).

Let's assume you're in good health, well-nourished, in good physical condition with a sound mind in a sound body. But your body does not like non-self-antigens, so it uses its natural ("innate") defenses like anatomical and chemical features (skin, tears, mucus membranes, anti-infectious barriers, enzymes) and a series of complex cellular elements. It's kind of a "yin and yang" metaphor where "self" is good and "non-self" (antigen) is evil.

Your body ("self") recognizes "non-self" (antigens) through a series of specialized white blood cells (WBCs or leukocytes, particularly macrophages, monocytes, and T-lymphocytes with their 'human leukocytic antigen [HLA]' receptors and CD4 surface proteins) that bind the antigen in an "antigen-presenting complex (APC)." This APC produces chemicals called cytokines (e.g., interferon, interleukins, IL-1, 4, 5, 6) that signal (signal #1) a series of T-helper, T-suppressor, and T-cytotoxic cells (Figure 2.1). Together this exquisite molecular biological process

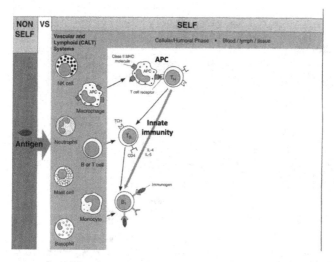

Figure 2.1 The innate (natural) immune response. (Louis J. Catania ©1996.)

called the innate immune system serves as the primary 24/7 defense of our health and wellness.[2] It truly is "our best friend."

CELLULAR AND HUMORAL (IMMUNOCHEMISTRY)

In a continuum of immune activity, in conjunction with the innate immune response, additional cellular elements (B-cells, B-idiotype cells, B-memory cells, plasma cells, natural killer [NK] cells) and more cytokines are continuously being generated to provide "memory" (B-memory cells) for future recognition and an "anamnestic" response to antigens. But more so, these additional cellular and chemical (humoral) elements are generating proteins called antibodies (specific to the invading antigen) and a complement system of immunoglobulin antibodies (IgA, IgG, IgM) which continue to bind and remove antigen through lysing, opsonization, chemotactic activity, and polymorphonuclear (PMN) phagocytosis. This form of immune activity is the first level of what is termed the adaptive (acquired) immune response (Figure 2.2).

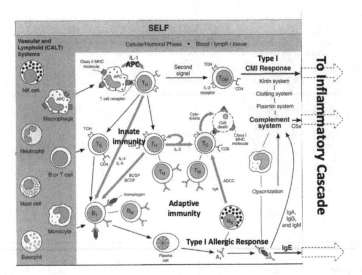

Figure 2.2 The adaptive (acquired) immune response. (Louis J. Catania ©1996.)

REVIEW OF AI FOR INNATE (NATURAL) IMMUNITY AND ACUTE INFLAMMATION

1   AI is being used in many immunological fields for its analytic abilities, antigen and phenotype (observable characteristics of an individual) detection, predicting prognosis and treatment outcomes, etc. Algorithms have been developed to predict the outcome of interactions and classification at molecular levels. Machine learning can predict genotypes (genetic composition) associated with poor prognosis.[3] Phenotype detection is another example of the classification abilities of AI being used for cellular phenotype detection and classification to determine the presence of a particular disease or its outcome. In certain diseases, the importance of phenotype classification at the molecular level is more prominent since it can directly determine prognosis and treatment plan. Image-based AI techniques (Section GPU, Chapter 1, Page 5) also have remarkable accuracy at both

cellular and molecular levels. Such image-based techniques have been recruited to determine immune responses such as macrophage activation[4] and lymphocyte infiltration in breast cancer and other solid tumors,[5] hence assist in determining prognosis and response to treatment. More studies have the potential to recruit AI and its analytic value in immunology.[6]

2 Potential regulatory mechanisms and identifying immunogenic prognostic markers for breast cancer (BC) were used to construct a prognostic signature for disease-free survival (DFS) of BC based on artificial intelligence algorithms. Differentially expressed immune genes were identified between normal tissues and tumor tissues. The artificial intelligence survival prediction system was developed based on three artificial intelligence algorithms. Comprehensive bioinformatics identified 17 immune genes as potential prognostic biomarkers, which might be potential candidates of immunotherapy targets in BC patients. These artificial intelligence survival predictive systems will be helpful to improve individualized treatment decision-making.[7]

3 Assessing antigen-induced T-cell activation is critical because only functionally active T-cells are capable of killing the desired targets. Autofluorescence imaging can distinguish T-cell activity states in a non-destructive manner by detecting endogenous changes in metabolic co-enzymes. However, recognizing robust activity patterns is challenging in the absence of exogenous labels. Machine learning has demonstrated methods that can accurately classify T-cell activity across human donors. Using cropped single-cell images from six donors, classifiers ranging from traditional models that use previously extracted image features to convolutional neural networks (CNNs) pre-trained on general non-biological images were studied. Adapting pre-trained CNNs for the T-cell activity classification task provides substantially better performance than traditional models or a simple CNN trained with the autofluorescence images alone.[8]

4 In Chapter 1 we stated the fact that, "The most effective data sources utilized in machine learning are graphics (video and

images)" and we referenced the graphic processing unit (GPU) by Nvidia as being responsible for that significant advance in AI. That advance led to multi-channel immunofluorescence imaging (cellular confocal microscopy) and cell membrane immunofluorescent stains with deep convolutional neural networks (DCNNs) to classify multiple T-cell and dendritic cell types. However, with densely packed cells, and complex image features, this technique reaches the limit and begins to produce poor image quality, and thus, the technique fails. It is at this limit that deep learning approaches excel. Using deep learning region-based segmentation techniques, it is now possible to analyze challenging image data that previously required laborious hand segmentation, based on multichannel information difficult for the human visual system to parse.[9]

5   AI enables radical new solutions to complex unsolved problems. As such, it is gaining momentum within the public health field. An overview of the current application of artificial intelligence (AI) in the field of public health and epidemiology focused on antimicrobial resistance, a topic of vital importance and included in the "Ten threats to global health in 2019" report published by the World Health Organization. Random mutations can make some bacteria immune to specific drugs, yet the widespread use of these drugs make these immune-modulated bacteria proliferate and, with resistance traits, they can be transferred among bacteria of different taxonomic and ecological groups. In other words, resistance can spread.[10] AI can help in two aspects: first, create a peptide structure (potent broad-spectrum antibiotics) to predict the degree of antimicrobial activity; and second, suggest new synthetic peptide structures as specific antimicrobial. Several authors have applied standard data mining models, including support vector machines (SVM) and artificial neural networks with results reaching an accuracy in the discrimination of antimicrobial versus non-antimicrobial peptides of 91.9%, 94.76%, and 95.79%.[11] AI enables radical new solutions to these complex unsolved public health problems.[12]

ADAPTIVE (ACQUIRED) IMMUNITY

Fundamentally, as described above, your innate immune system is all about the battle of self-versus non-self-antigens. Wouldn't it be nice if our body won all the battles? Needless to say, life doesn't work that way. Sometimes, the innate immune system can't quite handle the load. Maybe, for some pathological or environmental reason your system is compromised ("immunocompromised") or weakened or suppressed ("immunosuppression"). Perhaps the antigen is not being removed (persistent cause), or it keeps reoccurring (re-exposure) as the innate system tries to eliminate it. Or maybe the antigen is too abundant or too pernicious (virulent) for the innate immune response to overcome it. In such conditions, after a few days to a week of feeling "not so great," the strength of the human immune system begins to sdemonstrate a more aggressive "adaptive immune response." All in all, this adaptive immune system is a powerful defender and protector *to a point*.

Adaptive immunity is more vigorous than the innate form and control of its intensity and duration is poorly understood with genetic predisposition and three specific mechanisms believed to be inter-related. First is "feedback inhibition" where removal of the antigen reduces stimulus and thus decreased production of antibodies and cytokines, effectively reducing and reversing the response. Second is when T-suppressor cells reduce T-helper cells and thus a commensurate reduction of B-cell activity (controlled by T-helper cells). And third, the very complex system of idiotype antigen-specific B-cells increasing through genetic cloning and creating their own immunogenic stimuli which induces anti-idiotype-specific antibodies ("antibodies 1, 2") that establish an antibody idiotype-specific regulatory circuit. (This later process is why I mentioned "poorly understood" as this "regulatory circuit" remains the center of much immunology research which will be discussed further in Chapter 3, page 46).

Failure to remove the offending antigen in a timely manner, or malfunction of any one of the three mechanisms described above, can lead to an uncontrolled response resulting in acute inflammation (discussed below), chronic inflammation (Chapter 3), or a condition referred to as a "cytokine storm" which has potentially devastating consequences (as demonstrated in SARS-CoV-2 infections – discussed in Chapter 5). These phenomena and the endpoints of adaptive immunity represent the second half of our earlier stated paradox about the immune system. It can indeed be our worst enemy.

ACUTE INFLAMMATION

We can look at adaptive immunity as a race to eliminate the "bad guys" (antigens), a competition which, in most cases (given an otherwise healthy person), it wins. If, however, the underlying health of the patient (note how I move from "person" to "patient" here), is not adequate to sustain the activity of the adaptive immune response, things could begin to deteriorate or "dysregulate."

PATHOPHYSIOLOGY

As we described above, the adaptive immune response is using a lot of tools, i.e., cellular components and chemicals (cytokines) in amounts not normal ("pathophysiological") to your body. Their regular ("physiological") activity is working diligently to resolve the "pathological" (disease) process in your body, but those efforts are also producing abnormal chemical byproducts called "pro-inflammatory cytokines." Accumulation of these byproducts is a basis for the pathophysiological process called "acute inflammation." (Note: All inflammation, acute and chronic is characterized in medical terminology by the suffix "...itis." Thus, any condition mentioned, henceforth, under any disease category with the suffix "...itis" should be considered an inflammation.)

Acute inflammation is an efficient, though non-specific immunopathological defense mechanism of the adaptive immune system that produces an observable clinical response referred to as the "inflammatory cascade." The left side of the diagram in Figure 2.3 represents the pharmacodynamics most associated with acute inflammation and its medical treatment. You'll notice how the drug therapies

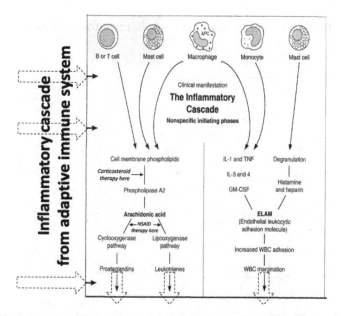

Figure 2.3 The inflammatory cascade. (Louis J. Catania ©1996.)

(corticosteroids and NSAIDs) at particular sites within the pharmacologic tree block pathways that lead to vasodilation (cyclooxygenase and lipoxygenase pathways), the first level of acute inflammation and pain (prostaglandins). Also, the chemicals (histamine and heparin) and mast cell molecule degranulation associated with the Type I allergic hypersensitivity reaction (described below) are immunomodulated within the pharmacological tree (right side). The balance of the biochemistry and molecular biology in this pharmacological diagram (right side) relates more to chronic inflammation and their relevance will be described in some detail in Chapter 3.

Acute inflammation can occur anywhere, internally or externally producing the inflammatory cascade. The "cascade" includes the pharmacological components producing inflammation and their subsequent clinical manifestations. The pathophysiology and histopathology of acute inflammation as defined in the inflammatory cascade is produced by the cells and mediators of the adaptive immune response

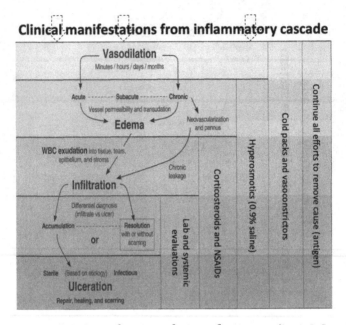

Figure 2.4 Clinical manifestations of acute inflammation. (Louis J. Catania ©1996.)

resulting in a dynamic unfolding of clinical events (Figure 2.4). The observable signs and symptoms that flow in the cascade include vasodilation ("rubor" or redness); edema or swelling ("tumor"); increased tissue or body temperature ("calor"); and pain ("dolor"). Cellular (leukocyte) accumulation ("infiltration") can lead to eventual tissue destruction ("ulceration") with loss of tissue or organ function ("functio laesa") and permanent tissue damage (scarring).

HYPERSENSITIVITY REACTIONS (TYPE I–IV)

Among the cellular reactions associated with the adaptive immune response, there are four classic "types" of clinical reactions produced by certain antigen categories and characterized by specific cellular responses and types of immunoglobulin antibodies (see Figure 2.2).

Type II (cytotoxic), III (immune-complex), and IV (cell-mediated, delayed reaction) are specific to certain antigens. Type I, the immediate, allergic (or anaphylactic) hypersensitivity response is produced by an antigen referred to as an "allergen." Examples of this response include hay fever, eczema, hives, asthma, food allergy, insect bites and stings, dust, pollen, and on and on. Like its antigen cousin, the allergen can be inhaled, ingested, or enter through the skin.

After a susceptible person is exposed to an allergen, the body starts producing a large quantity of IgE antibodies. This results in the reoccurrence of the allergic response, sometimes with increasing intensity with each re-exposure to the allergen. Included among its cytokines, are histamine and heparin (mentioned above), which along with other inflammatory symptoms, produces itching. With the allergic and hypersensitivity response, symptoms can also include, sneezing, and congestion (from histamine release and degranulation of mast cells – in Figure 2.3). In their most severe form, allergy or hypersensitivity can produce a life-threatening condition call anaphylaxis and anaphylactic shock.[13]

The clinical presentations in acute inflammation usually occur in hours to days (minutes in Type I immediate, allergic IgE response) and ulceration shortly thereafter if left untreated. Somewhat ironic in this sequence of the clinical inflammatory process, is that all of the effects up to (but not including) ulceration, are actually part of the immune system's healing process (bit of a "best friend – worst enemy" combination!).

CLINICAL CONSIDERATIONS IN ACUTE INFLAMMATION

The variety of treatment considerations (manipulations of the pharmacology in Figure 2.3) related to the inflammatory cascade is extensive, but the first treatment is always the removal of the cause (the antigen). Such removal can range from simple hygiene; to antibiotics or antivirals for a bacterial or viral infectious antigen, respectively (external or internal). Type I reactions (allergy) include removal of the allergen with the supportive therapy of antihistamine, decongestants, and mast cell stabilizing drugs. In more severe reactions (including anaphylaxis), corticosteroids and injectable epinephrine may be required. In all forms of acute inflammation, cold (wet or ice) compresses are enormously valuable to reduce inflammatory edema by producing vasoconstriction and reducing the vasodilation of associated blood vessels (i.e., rubor with tumor or edema) that are supplying inflammatory WBCs (diapedesis) to the effected site.

Topical and systemic corticosteroids are used to mitigate signs and symptoms in more acute inflammatory reactions. These drugs produce "masking effects" (reduction of signs and symptoms) but they are not curative as is sometimes thought. NSAIDs (non-steroidal anti-inflammatories such as aspirin, ibuprofen, or naproxen) provide pain relief (as anti-prostaglandins). Injury repair and stress reduction (physical, physiological, psychological) therapies are also valuable. Beyond these therapies, treatment is palliative and directed to the involved site (joint, muscle, internal organ, skin, etc.) to reduce the inflammatory process (assuming the antigen has been removed) and mitigate the pain. Additional measures include nutritional and vitamin supplements, omega-3 sources, compression, stress reduction, and exercise.

REVIEW OF AI FOR ADAPTIVE (ADAPTIVE) IMMUNITY AND ACUTE INFLAMMATION

1 As described in Chapter 1, "The most effective data sources utilized in machine learning are graphics (video and images)." The recognition of antigen by T-cells requires cell contact and is associated with changes in T-cell shape. By capturing these features in fixed tissue samples, in situ adaptive immunity could be quantified. A deep convolutional neural network (DCNN) was used to identify fundamental distance and cell-shape features associated with cognate help (cell-distance mapping (CDM)). In mice, CDM was comparable to excitation microscopy (TPEM) in discriminating cognate T-cell-dendritic cell (DC) interactions from non-cognate T-cell-DC interactions. This cell discrimination capability

through DCNN confirmed identification of antigen-presenting cells in certain diseases. This data provides a new approach with which to study human in situ adaptive immunity broadly applicable to autoimmunity, infection, and cancer.[14]

2   Diagnosis of acute appendicitis is challenging, especially due to the frequently unspecific clinical picture. Inflammatory blood markers and imaging methods like ultrasound are limited as they have to be interpreted by experts and still do not offer sufficient diagnostic certainty. A recent study presents a method for automatic diagnosis of appendicitis as well as the differentiation between complicated and uncomplicated inflammation using values/parameters which are routinely and unbiasedly obtained for each patient with suspected appendicitis. A total of 590 patients (473 patients with appendicitis in histopathology and 117 with negative histopathological findings) were analyzed retrospectively with modern algorithms from machine learning (ML) and artificial intelligence (AI). Results revealed the capability to prevent two out of three patients without appendicitis from useless surgery as well as one out of three patients with uncomplicated appendicitis. The presented method has the potential to change the current therapeutic approach for appendicitis and demonstrates the capability of algorithms from AI and ML to significantly improve diagnostics even based on routine diagnostic parameters.[15]

3   Cellular frustrated models can describe how the adaptive immune system works. They are composed by independent agents that continuously pair and unpair depending on the information that one subset of these agents display. The emergent dynamics is sensitive to changes in the displayed information and can be used to detect anomalies important to accomplishing the immune system's main function of protecting the host. Thus, these models could be adequate to model the immune system activation. It has been hypothesized that these models could provide inspiration to develop new artificial intelligence algorithms for data mining applications. Implementation strategies of these immune inspired ideas for anomaly

detection applications use real data to compare the performance of cellular frustration algorithms with standard implementations of one-class support vector machines and deep autoencoders. Results demonstrate that more efficient implementations of cellular frustration algorithms are possible and also that cellular frustration algorithms can be advantageous for semi-supervised anomaly detection applications given their robustness and accuracy.[16]

4 The inflammatory response runs through all stages of acne. It involves both innate and adaptive immunity. A study aimed to explore the candidate genes and their relative signaling pathways in inflammatory acne using data mining analysis. Aberrant differentially expressed genes (DEGs) and pathways involved in acne pathogenesis were identified using bioinformatic analysis. There were 12 DEGs identified and the pathways included chemokine signaling pathway, cytokine-cytokine receptor interaction, and Fc gamma R-mediated phagocytosis. The study could serve as a basis for further understanding the pathogenesis and potential therapeutic targets of inflammatory acne.

5 Using simulation experiments, an AI system called Multiple Shooting for Stochastic (randomly determined probability) Systems (MSS) method produced credible and prediction intervals with desired coverage in estimating key epidemic parameters (e.g., mean duration of infectiousness and R_0) and short- and long-term predictions (e.g., one- and three-week forecasts, timing and number of cases at the epidemic peak, and final epidemic size). In a humidity-based model susceptible members may be infected at a rate proportional to the prevalence of infectious individuals in the population and will immediately become infectious to others. Infectious individuals recover at a constant rate and develop temporary immunity against the circulating pathogen. Once the immunity wanes, the individual becomes susceptible to infection. A humidity-based stochastic compartmental influenza model accurately predicted influenza-like illness activity reported by U.S. Centers for Disease Control and Prevention from ten regions as well as city-level influenza activity using real-time, city-specific Google search query data.[17]

PATH TO CHRONIC INFLAMMATION

Through proper diagnosis and removal of the cause, in acute inflammation health and wellness will result. But, if not resolved within a reasonable period of time (weeks to months at most), the immune system advances to a condition called "chronic inflammation," different from acute inflammation in its cellular pathology and clinical symptoms (often none at all versus those of acute inflammation). It should also be noted that, though poorly understood, chronic inflammation can develop spontaneously, that is without an apparent antigen and acute inflammatory precursor episode.

This development of chronic inflammation could reasonably be considered an advanced form of acute inflammation. But its pathogenesis, histopathology, immunochemistry and particularly, its clinical course give cause to consider it as a distinct and unique clinical condition, notwithstanding its name. As such, let's address chronic inflammation (Chapter 3) as a distinct and separate disease entity, albeit often evolving from its "distant cousin," acute inflammation.

NOTES

1 Catania LJ. *Primary care of the anterior segment 2nd edition (textbook).* New York: McGraw Hill. Chapter 2. Clinical considerations on anterior segment pathology and immunology; January 1996. pp. 22–82.

2 The innate immune system. *Immunopaedia.* 2019.

3 Yu J, Hu Y, Xu Y, et al. An effective prediction model on prognosis of lung adenocarcinomas based on somatic mutational features. *BMC Cancer.* March 22, 2019;19(1):263.

4 Pavillon N, Hobro AJ, Akira S, et al. Noninvasive detection of macrophage activation with single-cell resolution through machine learning. *Proc Nat Acad Sci.* 2018;115(12):E2676–E2685.

5 Sun R, Limkin EJ, Vakalopoulou M, et al. A radiomics approach to assess tumour-infiltrating CD8 cells and response to anti-PD-1 or anti-PD-L1 immunotherapy: An imaging biomarker, retrospective multicohort study. *Lancet Oncol.* 2018;19(9):1180–1191.

6 Jabbari P, Rezaei N. Artificial intelligence and immunotherapy. *Expert Rev Clin Immunol.* 2019;5(7):689–691.

7   Zhang Z, Li J, He T, et al. Bioinformatics identified 17 immune genes as prognostic biomarkers for breast cancer: Application study based on artificial intelligence algorithms. *Front. Oncol.* March 31, 2020. doi: 10.3389/fonc.2020.00330.

8   Wang J, Walsh AJ, Skala C, et al. Classifying T cell activity in autofluorescence intensity images with convolutional neural networks. *J Biophotonics.* Augist 15, 2019. doi: 10.1002/jbio.201960050.

9   Sibley, AR. Investigating inflammation on the cellular level using machine learning. *Knowledge at University of Chicago.* December 20, 2019. doi: 10.6082/uchicago.2066.

10 Levy SB, Marshall B. Review antibacterial resistance worldwide: Causes, challenges and responses. *Nat Med.* December 2004;10(12 Suppl):S122–S129.

11 Youmans M, Spainhour C, Qiu P. Long short-term memory recurrent neural networks for antibacterial peptide identification. In: *2017 IEEE International Conference on Bioinformatics and Biomedicine (BIBM);* 2017. pp. 498–502.

12 Rodríguez-González A, Zanin M, Menasalvas-Ruiz E, et al. Public health and epidemiology informatics: Can artificial intelligence help future global challenges? An overview of antimicrobial resistance and impact of climate change in disease epidemiology. *Yearb Med Inform.* August 2019;28(1): 224–231.

13 Allergy and the immune system. *Johns Hopkins Health.* 2019.

14 Liarski VM, Sibley A, van Panhuys N, et al. Quantifying in situ adaptive immune cell cognate interactions in humans. *Nat Immunol.* April 2019;20:503–513. doi: 10.1038/s41590-019-0315-3.

15 Reismann J, Romualdi A, Kiss N, et al. Diagnosis and classification of pediatric acute appendicitis by artificial intelligence methods: An investigator-independent approach. *PLoS one.* September 25, 2019;14(9): 1–15.

16 Faria B, Vistulo de Abreu F. Cellular frustration algorithms for anomaly detection applications. *PLoS one.* July 8, 2019;14(7):e0218930.

17 Zimmer C, Leuba S, Cohen T, et al. Accurate quantification of uncertainty in epidemic parameter estimates and predictions using stochastic compartmental models. *Stat Methods Med Res.* December 2019;28(12):3591–3608.

3

AI AND CHRONIC
INFLAMMATION

INTRODUCTION

Think for a moment of the words you hear most frequently mentioned when listening to news on the coronavirus (don't include AI here quite yet, though it's ever-increasing in the COVID-19 discussion as we will demonstrate later in this chapter and in Chapter 5). Certainly, among your top choices would likely be "infection" and "inflammation." The reason is simple. The COVID-19 pandemic is caused by an "infectious" agent (i.e., SARS-CoV-2 or the novel coronavirus), but the clinical effects of the infection, "the disease" if you will, are a product of "inflammation," chronic inflammation to be exact. Whereas acute inflammation produces localized effects, ones which are usually manageable (per our Chapter 2 discussion), chronic inflammation is a diffuse process, one affecting any (and oftentimes, all) biological tissue(s) or organ system(s) in the body. Generally, it is difficult to treat, indeed impossible without removal of the cause (as exemplified in the case of COVID-19, the coronavirus), when possible.

As we emphasized in Chapter 2, the only effective way to cure a disease caused by an antigen is to identify (i.e., diagnose) and remove the antigen. In some cases, the adaptive immune response is itself successful in eliminating the antigen (self-resolution) and the disease state regresses toward normal. This will also reduce the active immune process with or without residual tissue or organ damage depending on intensity and duration of the persistent inflammatory state. Short of antigen removal and resolution of the disease process (chronic inflammation), one of five prevailing possibilities is the likely resultant etiology. First, the diagnosis was incorrect and the antigen was, in fact not removed. Second, there is an abnormality (mutation) in the patient's genome making them susceptibility to dysregulation of their immune system. Third, there is chronic exposure to environmental factors (e.g., toxins, pollution, smoking, etc.) which serve as a recurring stimulus to inflammation. Fourth, accumulating inflammatory byproducts of cellular and humoral components (pro-inflammatory cytokines) result in a persistent inflammatory stimulus. And finally, the causative antigen may be a disruption in homeostasis (e.g., stress); an innate, unknown autoantigenic factor; or "rogue" undeterminable APCs (antigen-presenting complex).[1] In the case of this later undeterminable cause or rogue APC, the disease process is considered to be an autoimmune disorder. These five etiologies and the pathogenesis of chronic inflammation are relevant to autoimmune disease and as such will be discussed more fully in Chapter 4, "AI and Autoimmunity."

PATHOGENESIS OF CHRONIC INFLAMMATION

One can ask at this point in a discussion on immunology, "So, other than duration, what's the difference between acute inflammation and chronic inflammation?" The differences are significant enough to consider chronic inflammation a distinct and separate disease entity from acute inflammation. They include: (1) a difference in the histopathology between the two; (2) a difference between the pharmacology and pharmacodynamics between the two; and (3) perhaps of greatest consequence, a dramatic difference between the clinical course, beyond duration, of acute versus chronic inflammatory disease. Let's look at each of these differences more closely to demonstrate the uniqueness of chronic versus acute inflammation. The only common resource material we will use in this discussion, both from Chapter 2, will be Figures 2.3 (page 23) and to a lesser degree, Figure 2.4 (page 24).

HISTOPATHOLOGY

First, let's consider the histopathological differences between acute and chronic inflammation. As opposed to acute inflammation, chronic inflammation includes unique histopathological tissue changes, not necessarily to the exclusion of their corresponding, precipitating pathological counterparts from the acute form (Figure 3.1). In chronic inflammation, edema and neovascularization produce swelling and hardening of the tissue (induration) as cell junctures loosen and produce cell and fluid migration through blood vessel walls (diapedesis) allowing inflammatory substances (cells and byproducts) to continue to accumulate in the tissue. Localized accumulation of monocytes, lymphocytes, neutrophils (WBCs), giant cells (granulomas) from the inflammatory response convert to fibroblasts producing further tissue induration and fibrinization. Granulomatous changes (areas of inflammation) produce loss of tissue function. Meanwhile, caseation, necrosis, and apoptosis (programmed cell death)[2] is disrupting and destroying tissue. Associated with all of these cellular dysfunctions is resultant molecular biologic immunogenomic and proteomic disturbances[3] (disruption of the cellular proteome, the normal cellular proteins expressed by the human genome[4] and the immunome, all the genes and proteins that constitute the immune system).[5] You can see that the magnitude of the histopathological changes in chronic inflammation are ominous and all-inclusive.

Finally, the clinical course of chronic inflammation distinguishing it from acute inflammation, beyond duration, is the magnitude of its pathological consequences on the body at large. According to most medical experts, chronic inflammatory disease is the progenitor or originating cause of all the major human disease categories (Figure 3.2). The clinical basis for this thesis lies in the diffuse and

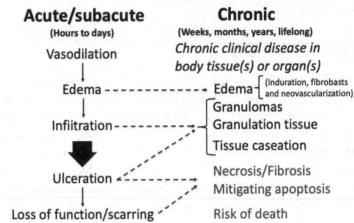

Figure 3.1 Acute versus chronic inflammation. (Louis J. Catania ©1996.)

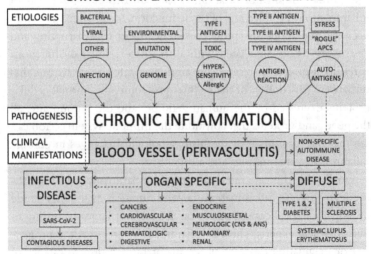

Figure 3.2 Chronic inflammation and disease. (Louis J. Catania ©1996.)

destructive nature of the chronic inflammatory process. As opposed to the acute inflammatory reaction, being a localized tissue process, in chronic inflammation the persistent inflammatory mediators and cellular components damage tissue locally (e.g., psoriasis, arthritis), in specific organ systems (e.g., Crohn's disease, glomerulonephritis), or throughout the body (e.g., vasculitis, diabetes and COVID-19 — more in Chapter 5).

Perhaps, the most devastating pathologic change in chronic inflammation is the invasion of the blood vessel walls (adventitia and endothelium) with associated vasodilation, increase in blood flow, capillary permeability (diapedesis as described above and in Chapter 2), and migration of neutrophils into the effected tissue through the inflamed capillary walls (perivasculitis). This results in infiltration of the primary inflammatory cells such as macrophages, lymphocytes, and plasma cells in the tissue site, producing inflammatory cytokines, growth factors, enzymes, and contributing to the progression of tissue damage and secondary repair (aka scarring) including fibrosis and granuloma formation. This effect compromises the tissue(s) and organ system(s), especially the cardiovascular system that the blood vessels supply.

As described above, over time, the tissues and organs, and even the DNA of their cells begin to break down, producing loss of bodily integrity, tissue proteomes, proteomics, and the immunome. These changes manifest themselves as recognizable chronic diseases. And to reemphasize, all of these devastating clinical changes occur diffusely in individual body tissues and organ systems throughout the body, thus the potential basis for all diseases.

PHARMACODYNAMICS

The second difference between acute and chronic inflammation is equally profound clinically. It relates to the pharmacology (cytokines, chemotactic factors, enzymes, hormones, proteoglycans, and reactive molecules) of the inflammatory cascade controlled by complex neurogenic and non-neurogenic mechanisms (see the right side of

Figure 2.3, page 23 in Chapter 2). It should be noted here that the drug-related immunotherapies that we will discuss here in relationship to chronic inflammation will apply as well to the autoimmune diseases to be discussed in Chapter 4. In fact, the pathogenesis of all autoimmune diseases discussed in Chapter 4 is the same pathogenesis described here for chronic inflammation. Simply stated, autoimmune diseases are the clinical manifestations of the pathogenesis of chronic inflammation (see Figure 3.2).

The immune cascade is a complex of pharmacologic agents (cellular and humoral) as well as molecular biologic elements (molecules and leukocytes) interacting to produce immunochemical responses (pharmacodynamics) that drive the immune response. The Figure 2.3 diagram in Chapter 2, page 23, represents only a portion of the elements involved. Table 3.1[6] is a limited list of pharmacologic, pro-inflammatory mediators (and their actions) used to immunomodulate the mechanisms that drive the pharmacodynamics of chronic inflammation. The basis of medical therapies for chronic inflammation (and its associated diseases including the autoimmune diseases) is the immunomodulation (amplifications, supplementation, suppression) of these chemical and molecular components to elicit therapeutic effects (immunotherapies).

The immune cells discussed in Chapter 2 (macrophages, monocytes, etc.) release cytokines such as IL-1, 3, 4 and tumor necrosis factor (TNF-α), a cytokine protein responsible for a wide range of signaling events within cells that lead to necrosis or apoptosis. Whereas this TNF-α protein is a potent pro-inflammatory cytokine, it also has been identified as having an important role in the resistance of infection and cancers. This dichotomy of actions presents therapeutic challenges in inhibiting TNF's inflammatory effects while protecting its beneficial anti-infection and anti-cancer properties. To wit, you'll notice numerous biologics in Table 3.2 directed at TNF inhibition (Orencia®, Humira®, Plaquenil®, Simponi®, Remicade®) to allow for alternate drug selections in an effort to maximize inflammatory inhibition while minimizing suppression of TNF's anti-infectious, anti-cancer properties. (More on TNF-α in the AI review below.)

Table 3.1 Pro-Inflammatory Mediators

Inflammatory Mediator (Label)	# of Types	Action
Histamine (H)	10	Vasodilation, smooth muscle contraction, pain, itching
Serotonin (S)	3	Vasodilation, smooth muscle contraction, pain
Bradykinin (B)	3	Vasodilation, smooth muscle contraction, pain
Complement (C)	4	Vasodilation, vasoconstriction, smooth muscle contraction, mast cell degranulation
Leukotriene (LT)	4	Vasodilation, vasoconstriction, smooth muscle contraction, chemotaxis
Prostaglandin (PG)	4	Vasodilation, pain
Fibrinopeptides (F)	1	Vasodilation
Interleukin (IL)	6	Stem cell proliferation, chemotaxis, lysozyme granule release, endothelial cell adhesion, granuloma formation, fever
Tumor necrosis factor (TNF-α)	2	Endothelial cell adhesion, granuloma formation, fever
Colony-stimulating factor (CSF) Granulocyte (G) Granulocyte macrophage (GM) Macrophage (M)	3	Stem cell proliferation
Platelet-activating factor (PAF)	3	Chemotaxis, lysozyme granule release, platelet aggregation
Tranexamic acid (TXA)	2	Smooth muscle contraction, platelet aggregation

Source: Louis J. Catania ©1996.

Table 3.2 Examples of Biologic Immunopharmacotherapeutics

Brand Name	Mechanism
Orencia®	T-cell inhibitor
Humira®	TNF inhibitor
Azasan®	Purine synthesis inhibitor
Plaquenil®	Suppression of IL-1 and TNF-α, induce apoptosis of inflammation cells and decrease chemotaxis
Sandimmune®	Calcineurin inhibitor
Enbrel®	TNF inhibitor
Simponi®	TNF inhibitor
Remicade®	TNF inhibitor
Arava®	Pyrimidine synthesis inhibitor
Trexall®	Purine metabolism inhibitor
Minocin®	5-LO inhibitor
Rituxan®	Monoclonal antibody
Azulfidine®	Suppression of IL-1 and TNF-α-

Source: Louis J. Catania ©1996.

This complex of cytokines induce endothelial leukocytic adhesion molecules (ELAMs) which stimulate leukocytic (WBC neutrophils) adhesion and cellular migration associated with blood vessel wall permeability and diapedesis. Once the circulating leukocytes migrate to the disease site(s), they are activated by various cytokines and chemokines secreted by the macrophages and dendritic cells. On activation, the leukocytes release additional cytokines and mediators of inflammation. Meanwhile, neutrophils (WBCs) are also helping to destroy the antigen by phagocytosis through the release of reactive oxygen species. Cytokines such as IL-1, IL-6, and TNF-α, T-lymphocytes, and B-lymphocytes are an additional line of defense by mediating inflammation through several complex mechanisms including secreting of cytokines and production of antibodies and immune complexes. Circulating platelets also play a role in this pharmacodynamic process by platelet aggregation, thrombus formation, and degranulation releasing chemokines and inflammatory mediators.[7]

These complex pharmacodynamics in the inflammatory process are presented here to illustrate the basis of immunotherapies for chronic inflammation as well as all of its associated clinical conditions including the autoimmune diseases associated with infectious diseases and cancers. These immunotherapies will be discussed below under "Treatment" and expanded upon further in Chapter 4's discussion on "Treatment for autoimmune diseases."

REVIEW OF AI FOR THE PATHOGENESIS OF CHRONIC INFLAMMATION

One can make a categorical statement that all AI addressing chronic inflammation applies to autoimmune diseases as well. As such, it would be worthwhile to review both related sections on AI applications in Chapters 3 and 4 as you read these literature thumbnails. (I will repeat this statement in reverse, in Chapter 4 as well.)

1   Recent research[8] has revealed that certain social, environmental, and lifestyle factors can promote systemic chronic inflammation (SCI) that can, in turn, lead to several diseases such as cardiovascular disease, cancer, diabetes mellitus, chronic kidney disease, non-alcoholic fatty liver disease, and autoimmune and neurodegenerative disorders. Chronic inflammatory diseases have been recognized as the most significant cause of death in the world today, with more than 50% of all deaths being attributable to inflammation-related diseases.[9] It is proving useful in applying multi-omics approaches, computational modeling, and artificial intelligence to study how SCI-related mechanisms both change and predict changes in clinical status within individuals over the life span[10].

2   Activation of inflammatory processes likely leads to changes in gait, posture, and mobility patterns. A machine learning (ML)

study was conducted to determine the effect of inflammation on gait and motion in humans. During inflammation, compared to a control group, participants exhibited shorter, slower, and wider strides, less arm extension, less knee flexion, and a more downward-tilting head while walking. They were also slower and took a shorter first step in the timed-up-and-go test. Higher interleukin-6 concentrations, stronger sickness symptoms, and lower body temperature predicted the inflammation-related alterations in biological motion. These findings show that biological motion contains clear information about the inflammatory status of an individual, and may be used by peers or artificial intelligence to recognize that someone is sick or contagious.[11]

3 AI mainly focuses on evaluating the treatment effects to help physicians adjust treatment plans in cancer immunotherapy. An AI platform was developed based on machine learning to accurately predict the therapeutic effect of programmed cell death protein 1 (PD-1) inhibitors. The platform effectively evaluated the effect of immunotherapy in patients with advanced solid tumors who are sensitive to PD-1 checkpoint inhibitors. This machine learning method based on human leukocyte antigen (HLA) mass spectrometry database improves the identification of cancer neoantigen and improves the efficacy of cancer immunotherapy.[12]

4 In Crohn's disease or ulcerative colitis, TNF (tumor necrosis factor α) appears to be a major inflammation-promoting and tissue damage-promoting effector molecule. Besides its role in inflammation and cell death, TNF presents a wide range of pleiotropic (one gene influencing others) activities with implications in various cellular processes, including proliferation and differentiation. Research is being conducted studying the molecular mechanisms and their potential crosstalk that regulate the different TNF-initiated cellular outcomes in the intestine, as well as possible applications for pharmacological interventions in the treatment of inflammatory disorders of the intestinal mucosa.[13]

5 Inflammation is a hallmark of many health conditions, but quantifying how the underlying biology of inflammation contributes

to specific diseases has been difficult. For the first time, UNC School of Medicine researchers and colleagues now report the development of a new technology to identify neutrophils that are primed to eject inflammatory DNA into the circulation via a process called NETosis. Using convolutional neural networks (CNNs), machine learning (ML) is being used to perform classification and quantitation of images of nuclei from human blood neutrophils.[14]

CLINICAL DIAGNOSIS AND TREATMENT OF CHRONIC INFLAMMATION

DIAGNOSTIC STRATEGIES

As opposed to acute inflammation, chronic inflammation can be difficult to identify, especially in situations where no precipitating cause (acute inflammation, antigenic, or otherwise) exists. Given the all-inclusive nature of chronic inflammation as an immunological disease, its diagnosis can be organ-specific or disseminated among multiple body systems (see Figure 3.2). The diagnostic evaluation includes a thorough history, physical examination, laboratory testing, and imaging based on suspected organ-system involvement(s). In all the cases, signs and symptoms can vary widely.

Generally speaking, patients with chronic diseases can be somewhat de facto assumed to have some degree of chronic inflammation. The Center for Disease Control (CDC) defines chronic diseases as "conditions that last one year or more and require ongoing medical attention or limit activities of daily living or both."[15] Chronic diseases such as heart disease, cancer, and diabetes also are the leading causes of death and disability in the United States and are the leading drivers of the nation's $3.5 trillion in annual health care costs. No surprise when considering the prevalence of chronic diseases. Six in ten adults in the United States have a chronic disease. Four in ten have two or more (comorbidities).[16] While there are significant numbers of disease states that can be classified as chronic, Table 3.3 lists the ten most common chronic conditions

Table 3.3 Ten Most Common Chronic Conditions (Ranked By Death Rate)

---

1. Heart disease (death rate 23.0%)
2. Cancer (death rate 21.3%)
3. Unintentional injury (death rate 6%)
4. Respiratory diseases including asthma and COPD (death rate 5.7%)
5. Stroke and cerebrovascular disease (death rate of 5.2%)
6. Alzheimer's disease (death rate of 4.3%)
7. Type 2 Diabetes (death rate 3%)
8. Influenza and pneumonia (death rate 2%)
9. Kidney disease (death rate 1.8%)
10. Chronic liver disease and cirrhosis (death rate 1.8%)

Source: National Vital Statistics Reports. June 24, 2019;68(6).

ranked by death rate. Such prioritized lists vary based on demographic factors (i.e., age, gender, race, geographic location, and socioeconomics):[17] Notwithstanding such demographic considerations, as mentioned previously, "...chronic inflammatory disease is the progenitor or originating cause of all the major chronic disease categories."

Not included in Table 3.3 of chronic diseases is obesity (BMI > 25mg/kg^2). When given the CDC's definition (above) of chronic disease and current epidemiological data on obesity (prevalence, 40.0% among young adults aged 20–39 years, 44.8% among middle-aged adults aged 40–59 years, and 42.8% among adults aged 60 and older) as well as an increase of 11.9% from 1999 to 2018,[18] obesity must be considered a chronic disease, perhaps the leading chronic disease. Sadly, this major disease risk factor (obesity) associated with chronic inflammation significantly increases the morbidity and mortality of chronic diseases and now, for COVID-19[19] (more discussion on this in Chapter 5). The prevalence of comorbidities with obesity reach levels as high as 52.3% with common conditions such as hypertension and diabetes and a corresponding increases in the mortality rates.[20]

Non-specific symptoms associated with chronic inflammation include:

- Body pain, arthralgia, myalgia;
- Chronic fatigue and insomnia;
- Depression, anxiety, and mood disorders;
- Gastrointestinal complications like constipation, diarrhea, and acid reflux;
- Weight gain or weight loss;
- Frequent infections;
- Fatigue;
- Fever;
- Mouth sores;
- Rashes;
- Abdominal pain;
- Chest pain.

Unfortunately, there are no absolute, specific laboratory tests to assess patients for chronic inflammation. In fact, such tests are generally undertaken when the inflammation occurs in association with another medical condition (comorbidity). Some of these laboratory tests include serum protein electrophoresis (SPE), C-reactive protein (CRP), and erythrocyte sedimentation rate (ESR).

TREATMENT (IMMUNOMODULATING THERAPIES)

Chronic inflammation and autoimmune diseases often require treatment directed at the tissue(s) and organ system(s) being adversely affected. Some of those organ-specific treatments are used in conditions related directly and indirectly to chronic inflammation and autoimmunities including cancers, Type 1 diabetes, and many other autoimmune diseases. More generalized treatment falls under the category of immunosuppressive and immunomodulating (suppressing or stimulating) therapies, sometimes referred to as "non-specific therapies." These therapies include types of drugs (examples in Table 3.2) that are used to suppress immune system's auto-antigenicity in autoimmune diseases or to boost the immune system response in cancers and anti-tumor therapies.

Treatment for chronic inflammation must be directed at the multiple tissue(s) and organ system(s) being affected. Thus, such treatment is usually delivered through non-specific, broad-based systemic drugs. Indeed, there are targeted immunotherapeutic procedures for chronic inflammation in the forms of stem cell transplantation, and immunogenetic and immunogenomic therapies, all of which shall be presented in Chapter 4. In this section, we will focus on the immunopharmacotherapeutics (i.e., pharmacologic immunomodulation) and their related AI applications targeted at the cellular, biochemical, and molecular biological processes occurring in chronic inflammation and discussed above under pharmacodynamics.

Standard treatments used for acute inflammation (steroids, NSAIDs discussed in Section "Acute Inflammation", Chapter 2, Page 22) are of some value in chronic inflammation, but rarely prove adequate for maximal therapy (although the corticosteroid dexamethasone is proving to be of some value in COVID-19 – more in Chapter 5). Rather, the principal approach in treating chronic inflammation is obviously to suppress those immunochemical and molecular biologic processes (right side of Figure 2.3) that are promoting inflammatory (pro-inflammatory cytokine) changes and conversely, to stimulate and promote those agents that inhibit the inflammatory process (see Tables 3.1 and 3.2). In some cases, drugs are used for these dual purposes and sometimes the actual cells and chemicals (humoral agents) involved in a bodily process are used to supplement the body's own defense mechanisms. As an example, monoclonal antibodies (any drug with the name suffix, "...mab") are laboratory-engineered antibodies used to mimic the immune system's own antibodies for a specific antigen and its resultant chronic inflammation (see also Chapter 5, page 106).

Among the two categories of immunomodulating drugs, in the immunosuppressive category there is a group termed "disease-modifying anti-rheumatic drugs (DMARDs)."[21] These include drugs such as hydroxychloroquine (Plaquenil®, you've heard of that one, I'm sure!), methotrexate, sulfasalazine, and leflunomide. Second are the "biologic drugs,"[22] which are a category that is attempting to regulate (increase or decrease) the immune response. These biologics are non-specific (or generic) for the range of diseases produced from chronic inflammation, and act on the pharmacology to biochemically inhibit pro-inflammatory agents or promote inhibitory agents. Among these biologics are a large number of drug options including etanercept, adalimumab, abatacept, and many others, some listed in Table 3.2 with their immunomodulating mechanisms. Some more of the popular non-specific immunotherapeutic agents include cytokines like interferons; interleukins; anti-TNF (tumor necrosis factor, a pro-inflammatory cytokine); gene-based delivery systems; and other immune system modulators.

Checkpoint inhibitors are monoclonal antibody drugs that target and attach to PD-1, PD-L1, and CTLA-4, (anti-cancer) proteins on T-cells (and some cancer cells). This binding action can inhibit the proteins and boost the immune response against cancer cells. These drugs are given intravenously and have been shown to be helpful in treating several types of cancer with new cancer types being added as more studies show the drugs to be effective. Examples of drugs that target PD-1 include Pembrolizumab (Keytruda®), Nivolumab (Opdivo®), and Cemiplimab (Libtayo®). PD-L1 drugs include Atezolizumab (Tecentriq®), Avelumab (Bavencio®), and Durvalumab (Imfinzi®). Ipilimumab (Yervoy®) is a CTLA-4 checkpoint inhibitor and is used specifically to treat skin melanoma. Some common side effects of checkpoint inhibitors include diarrhea, pneumonitis (inflammation in the lungs), rashes and itchiness, problems with some hormone levels, and kidney infections.[23]

The reason for the large variety of drugs is due to the extensive amount of pro-inflammatory mediators in the chronic inflammatory and autoimmune process.[24] Additionally, researchers have found a new way to treat the inflammation involved in chronic diseases such as psoriasis, asthma, and HIV. A group of transmitter substances (cytokines) in the immune system, the so-called IL-1 family (see Chapter 2,

Figure 2.2), has been shown to play an important role in many of these diseases by regulating APCs and the body's immune responses.[25]

While the biologics include a large number of drug options, all are attempting to regulate (increase or decrease) the immune response. Each has a distinct biochemical effect on different mediators. This gives treating physicians the option of "experimenting" with a variety of biologics to get a maximal drug effect. It also confuses the hell out of the public (especially those using a biologic) when they watch a TV commercial promoting a biologic drug for a specific autoimmune condition (e.g., rheumatoid arthritis) on one station. Then they change channel and see the same drug being promoted for an entirely different condition (e.g., Crohn's Disease). The drugs are specific for individual mediators that occur in all of the autoimmune diseases, and thus, they are non-specific for any one disease.

Finally, you'll notice in Table 3.3 that cancer is one of the leading (#2) prevalent diseases associated with chronic inflammation. Of course, it is well established that the fundamental cause of cancer relates to genetic mutation(s) and in Chapter 4 we will be addressing therapeutic technologies being used in autoimmune disorders which are also being used extensively in cancer treatment. In fact, because of its high degree of incidence and prevalence, all immunotherapeutic agents (i.e., the biologics and non-specific agents) presented above and immunogenetic and genomic therapies (in Chapter 4) are being applied to cancer at the clinical and research levels. In that regard, one other interesting immunotherapeutic approach is receiving considerable attention in recent years. It pertains to the reference made back in Section "Adaptive (Acquired) Immunity" in Chapter 2 (page 21) about "... the very complex system of idiotype antigen-specific B cells" which is also referred to as the "idiotype network theory (INT)."[26]. It is being studied extensively as a potential cancer immunization therapy.

A brief summary of this complex theory starts with part of an antibody binding with a specific antigen. Then generated B-cells begin to produce genetically cloned antibodies with unique profiles of idiotypic epitopes (called idiotypes or antigen-binding sites for the cloned antibodies) that increase immunogenic stimulation. This stimulation induces anti-idiotype and anti-anti-idiotype antibodies (called antibody-2 and antibody-3, and beyond) which ultimately suppress continued stimulation by binding with compatible T suppressor cells. This binding produces a regulatory closed-loop suppressor system (or circuit) in the lymphoid system and provides antibodies which can eliminate a persistent antigen, in the case of cancer, the carcinogen or carcinogenic stimulus. These anti-idiotype antibodies have the potential to provide long-lasting immunity as a vaccine for cancer.[27] (I told you it was complex! But its potential benefits to our public health and humanity definitely earn it a place in this discussion.)

Postulating a universal disease etiology the magnitude of which we have identified chronic inflammation to be can easily be misinterpreted as an overzealous statement of the breadth and depth of chronic inflammation. To address such reasonable doubt, let's use immunoinformatics to defend the thesis by quoting a few perspectives on chronic inflammation from among thousands of authoritative journal articles over the past few years:

- Chronic inflammatory diseases are the most significant cause of death in the world. StatPearls. July 4, 2020.[28]
- Schofield A. Inflammation: The Root of All Disease. Vitalfit Collective. January 10, 2019.[29]
- "...inflammatory processes are involved in not just a few select disorders, but a wide variety of mental and physical health problems that dominate present-day morbidity and mortality worldwide." National Center for Biotechnology Information, U.S. National Library of Medicine. December 25, 2019.[30]
- "Indeed, chronic inflammatory diseases are the most significant cause of death in the world today, with more than 50% of all deaths being attributable to inflammation-related diseases." Washington Post Health. Jan. 20, 2020.[31]
- "Today, chronic inflammatory diseases are at the top of the list of death causes." Medical Press. January 29, 2020.[32]
- World Health Organization (WHO) ranks chronic diseases as the greatest threat to human health. WHO, July 27, 2018.[33]

Thus, per our stated paradox, immunology (specifically, chronic inflammation) is "our worst enemy." Sadly, COVID-19 is a painful example of this incongruity (see Chapter 5).

REVIEW OF AI FOR THE PATHOGENESIS OF CHRONIC INFLAMMATION

1   Anti-tumor necrosis factor (anti-TNF) drugs are an important second-line treatment for rheumatoid arthritis after methotrexate. However, patient heterogeneity hinders identification of predictive biomarkers and accurate modeling of anti-TNF drug responses. A study was conducted to investigate the usefulness of machine learning to assist in developing predictive models for treatment response. Using data on patient demographics, baseline disease assessment, treatment, and single-nucleotide polymorphism (SNP) array from the Dialogue on Reverse Engineering Assessment and Methods (DREAM): Rheumatoid Arthritis Responder Challenge, a Gaussian process regression model was developed to predict changes in the Disease Activity Score in 28 joints for the patients and to classify them into either the responder or the non-responder group. The method predicted changes with a correlation coefficient of 0.405 and correctly classified responses from 78% of patients. Gaussian process regression effectively remapped the feature space and identified subpopulations that do not respond well to anti-TNF treatments. This was the best-performing model in the DREAM Challenge.

2   Using common non-invasive techniques for body composition assessment methods (CT, MRI), images extracted by these methods can be processed with artificial intelligence (AI) and radiomic analysis. The idea is to suggest the use of AI applications and radiomic analysis to search for features that may be extracted from medical images [computed tomography (CT) and magnetic resonance imaging (MRI)], and that may turn out to be good predictors of metabolic disorder and chronic diseases like obesity and cancer. This could lead to patient-specific treatments and management of several diseases linked with excessive body fat.[34]

3   The generation of continuously collected large data sets from various molecular profiling (genetic, genomic, proteomic, epigenomic, and others) efforts of patient samples by the development and deployment of wearable medical devices (IoTs) and mobile health applications, and clinical outcome data has enabled the biomedical community to apply artificial intelligence (AI) and machine learning algorithms to vast amounts of data. The application of precision immunoprofiling by image analysis and artificial intelligence to biology and disease was demonstrated in a recent paper where the authors used immunoprofiling data to assess immuno-oncology biomarkers, such as PD-L1 (see also page 45) and immune cell infiltrates as predictors of patient's response to cancer treatment.[35]

4   The interplay between tumor and immune cells within the tumor microenvironment is increasingly important in the study of immuno-oncology. Before deep learning (DL), algorithms for tissue image analysis were often biologically inspired in collaboration with pathologists and required computer scientists to handcraft descriptive features for a computer to classify a certain type of tissue or cell. Now, machine learning (ML) allows for high-throughput generation of features that describe spatial relationships for thousands of cells, an infeasible task for pathologists. Improvements in individual cell and tissue detection via DL methods allow for very precise measurements of the tumor microenvironment, so heterogeneous features that describe spatial relationships between cells and tissue structures can now be measured at scale.[36]

5   Kynurenine pathway enzymes have been identified as key regulators of cancer immunity. An artificial intelligence (AI) with deep learning technology was employed to rationally design and discover a novel kynurenine pathway regulator with potent immunotherapeutic efficacy. The study demonstrated that AI modeling with deep learning is a valid strategy for a rational and effective development of an immunotherapeutic drug. This AI-based platform can be applied to other molecular targets to speed up the immuno-oncologic drug development.[37]

NOTES

1 Disease Development. How do autoimmune diseases unfold? *Johns Hopkins Medicine Pathology.* 2019.

2 Campanati A, Paolinelli M, Diotallevi F, et al. Pharmacodynamics OF TNF α inhibitors for the treatment of psoriasis. *Expert Opin Drug Metab Toxicol.* November2019;15(11):913–925.doi:10.1080/17425255.2019.1681969.

3 Cutolo M, Soldano S, Smith V. Pathophysiology of systemic sclerosis: Current understanding and new insights. *Expert Rev Clin Immunol.* July 2019;15(7):753–764.

4 What are proteomes? *Uniprot Consortium.* January 22, 2020.

5 Biancotto A, McCoy JP. Studying the human immunome: The complexity of comprehensive leukocyte immunophenotyping. *Curr Top Microbiol Immunol.* 2014;377:23–60. doi:10.1007/82_2013_336.

6 Proinflammatory cytokine list. *Sino Biological.* 2020.

7 Pahwa R, Goyal A, Bansal P, et al. Chronic inflammation. *StatPearls [Internet].* July 4, 2020.

8 Furman D, Campisi J, Verdin E, et al. Chronic inflammation in the etiology of disease across the life span. *Nat Med.* 2019;25:1822–1832. doi: 10.1038/s41591-019-0675.

9 GBD 2017 Causes of Death Collaborators. Global, regional, and national age-sex-specific mortality for 282 causes of death in 195 countries and territories, 1980–2017: A systematic analysis for the global burden of disease study 2017. *Lancet.* 2018;392:1736–1788.

10 Schüssler-Fiorenza Rose SM, et al. A longitudinal big data approach for precision health. *Nat Med.* 2019;25:792–804.

11 Lasselinabc J, Sundelinabd T, Waynee PM, et al. Biological motion during inflammation in humans. *Brain Behav Immun.* February 202084:147–153.

12 Lianga G, Fanb W, XiaoZhua HL. The emerging roles of artificial intelligence in cancer drug development and precision therapy. *Biomed. Pharmacother.* August 2020;128:110255.

13 Delgado ME, Brunner T. The many faces of tumor necrosis factor signaling in the intestinal epithelium. *Genes Immun.* 2019;20:609–626. doi: 10.1038/s41435-019-0057-0.

14 Elsherif L, Sciaky N, Carrington A, et al. Machine learning to quantitate neutrophil NETosis. *Sci Rep.* 2019;9(1). doi: 10.1038/s41598-019-53202-5.

15 About Chronic Diseases. National center for chronic disease prevention and health promotion. *CDC.* October 23, 2019.

16 Ibid. About Chronic Diseases. 15.

17 Heron M. Division of vital statistics. Deaths: Leading causes for 2017. *National Vital Statistics Reports.* June 24, 2019;68(6).

18 CDC. Adult obesity facts. Division of nutrition, physical activity, and obesity. *National Center for Chronic Disease Prevention and Health Promotion.* June 29, 2020.

19 Pennington Biomedical Research Center. Why is obesity so common in COVID-19 patients? *Medical Press.* July 24, 2020.

20 Nguyen NT, Magno CP, Lane KT, et al. Association of hypertension, diabetes, dyslipidemia, and metabolic syndrome with obesity: Findings from the *National Health and Nutrition Examination Survey,* 1999 to 2004. *J Am Coll Surg.* 2008;207(6):928–934.

21 Cohen S, Cannella A. Patient education: Disease-modifying antirheumatic drugs (DMARDs) (Beyond the Basics). *UpToDate.* February 28, 2019.

22 Ogbru O. Biologics (biologic drug class). *MedicineNet.* 2019.

23 Alteri R, Kalidas M. Immune checkpoint inhibitors and their side effects. *American Cancer Society.* December 27, 2019.

24 Mandal A. Autoimmune disease development of therapies. *News Medical Life Science.* May 29, 2019.

25 Falkesgaard Højen J, Vindvad Kristensen ML, McKee AS, et al. IL-1R3 blockade broadly attenuates the functions of six members of the IL-1 family, revealing their contribution to models of disease. *Nat Immunol.* 2019;20(9):1138. doi: 10.1038/s41590-019-0467-1.

26 Kohler H, Pashov A, Kieber-Emmons T. The promise of anti-Idiotype revisited. *Front. Immunol.* March 26, 2019;10:808. doi: 10.3389/fimmu.2019.00808.

27 Naveed A, Rahman SU, Arshad MI, et al. Recapitulation of the anti-Idiotype antibodies as vaccine candidate. *Transl Med Commun.* March 1, 2018;3:1. doi: 10.1186/s41231-018-0021-4.

28 Ibid. Pahwa. 7.

29 Schofield A. Inflammation: The root of all disease. *Vitalfit Collective.* January 10, 2019.

30 Furman D, Campisi J, Verdin E, et al. Chronic inflammation in the etiology of disease across the life span. *Nat Med.* December 2019;25(12):1822–1832. doi: 10.1038/s41591-019-0675-0.

31 Cimons M. Chronic inflammation is long lasting, insidious, dangerous. And you may not even know you have it. *Washington Post Health.* January 20, 2020.

32 Lobachevsky University. Scientists have identified the role of chronic inflammation as the cause of accelerated aging. *Medical Press.* January 29, 2020.

33 Han S. World Health Organization (WHO) ranks chronic diseases as the greatest threat to human health. *HealthLine.* July 27, 2018.

34 Attanasio S, Forte SM, Restante G, et al. Artificial intelligence, radiomics and other horizons in body composition assessment. *Quant Imaging Med Surg.* 2020;10(8):1650–1660. doi:10.21037/qims.2020.03.10.

35 Koelzer VH, Sirinukunwattana K, Rittscher J, et al. Precision immunoprofiling by image analysis and artificial intelligence. *Virchows Arch.* 2018. doi: 10.1007/s00428-018-2485-z.

36 Vamathevan J, Clark D, Czodrowski P, et al. Applications of machine learning in drug discovery and development. *Nat Rev Drug Discov.* 2019;18(6):463–477. doi: 10.1038/s41573-019-0024-5.

37 Lee WS, Kim JH, Lee HJ, et al. Artificial intelligence technology enables a rational development of a potent immunotherapeutic agent. *Proceedings of the Annual Meeting of the American Association for Cancer Research 2020;* June 22–24, 2020. Philadelphia (PA): AACR; *Cancer Res* 2020;80(16 Suppl):Abstract nr 2092.

4

AI AND AUTOIMMUNITY

INTRODUCTION

Antigens, by definition, are "foreign," but as we learn more about the immune system, it has become apparent that "foreign" may not be entirely synonymous with "non-self." When, for some unknown reason, the body incorrectly identifies itself (self) as foreign (i.e., "non-self," thus becoming an "autoantigen" and generating a process referred to as "autoantigenicity"), it initiates an adaptive immune response directed at itself. Stated another way, the immune system has the potential to produce an "autoimmune response."[1] Autoimmune disease develops after immune system dysregulation (see Chapter 2, page 22), in both the innate and adaptive immune systems.[2] This category of immune diseases occurs in females at a rate of greater than two to one over males[3] (6.4% of women versus 2.7% of men). Some theories as to why such a strong female predilection include male testosterone protection, pregnancy factors, and gene expression.[4] But regarding definitive etiologies of autoimmune diseases and their variable clinical features, exact causes remain unknown.

There are several theories as to the cause of this idiosyncratic response. But whatever the cause, the response has created an entirely separate disease category referred to as the "autoimmune diseases." Table 4.1 reveals an impressive (and ominous) list of prevalent autoimmune diseases. As mentioned previously in Chapter 3 and just above, notwithstanding the fact that the etiology of this disease

Table 4.1 Listing of Prevalent Autoimmune Diseases

• Ankylosing spondylitis	• Giant cell arteritis	• Graves' disease
• Lupus	• Temporal arteritis	• Guillain-Barré syndrome
• Rheumatoid arthritis	• Polymyalgia rheumatica	• Hashimoto's disease
• Juvenile arthritis	• Polyarteritis nodosa	• Hemolytic anemia
• Scleroderma	• Polymyositis	• Idiopathic thrombocytopenic purpura
• Dermatomyositis	• Takayasu arteritis	
• Behcet's disease	• Granulomatosis with polyangiitis	• Inflammatory bowel disease
• Celiac disease		
• Crohn's disease	• Vasculitis	
• Ulcerative colitis	• Alopecia areata	• Multiple sclerosis
• Sjogren's syndrome	• Antiphospholipid	• Myasthenia gravis
• Reactive arthritis	• Antibody syndrome	• Primary biliary cirrhosis
• Mixed connective tissue disease	• Autoimmune hepatitis	• Psoriasis
• Raynaud's phenomenon	• Type 1 diabetes	• Vitiligo

Source: Foundations of AI in and Bioscience; Catania; Academy Press. November 2020.

category remains unknown or at least open to multiple hypotheses, its pathogenesis and thus, its therapeutic strategies are similar to those of chronic inflammation in that chronic inflammation is the immunological process responsible for autoimmune diseases. Thus, rather than repeating extended descriptions of the pathogenesis and immunotherapies presented in Chapter 3, I will be referring numerous times throughout this chapter back to Chapter 3, "AI and Chronic Inflammation."

THEORIES OF PATHOGENESIS OF AUTOIMMUNE DISEASE

The cause(s) of autoimmune diseases remain unknown, but research has strongly suggested a pathogenesis ("natural history") of the

Table 4.2 Theories on Etiologies and Pathogenesis of Chronic Inflammation and Autoimmune Disease

---

1. A prolonged inflammatory process from failure to eliminate an antigen;
2. Part of the patient's genome;
3. Environmental factors to which patient is exposed over time;
4. Increasing release and accumulation of pro-inflammatory cytokines;
5. An abnormal immune response to "self":
   a. Disruption of homeostasis (*Yin Yang*);
   b. Innate autoantigens from inflammatory process;
   c. "*Rogue*" antigen-presenting cells (*APCs*)

Source: Foundations of AI in Healthcare and Bioscience; Catania; Academy Press. December 2020.

disease progression over time and the damage it produces. The path of the disease includes five possible (probable?) causes (Table 4.2) mentioned briefly in Chapter 3, page 32. Let's examine each of them as regards their suppositions and their factual basis.[5]

A PROLONGED INFLAMMATORY PROCESS FROM FAILURE TO ELIMINATE AN ANTIGEN

If everything in this world that is not "self" is antigenic to self, based on the discussion in Section "Innate (Natural) Immunity", Chapter 2, page 16, it would seem that the overwhelming percentage of antigenic attacks on self are controlled by our innate (natural) immunity (our "friend"). Occasionally, however, antigens are not removed in a timely fashion or continually reoccur through re-exposure, an example of which would be a persistent allergen (seasonal or otherwise). Inability to remove an antigen will continually stimulate the innate immune system with resultant accumulating cellular, humoral, molecular byproducts which begin to trigger the adaptive immune response. Notwithstanding a powerful and inclusive innate defense system, pathogenic antigens can breach this immune barrier and result in the adaptive immune response. Some of those pathogens prove to be virulent enough to resist or even overcome the body's adaptive response. In such cases, the immune system continues to "fight the fight," the results of which produces prolonged chronic inflammation and the clinical sequalae of that prolonged process resulting in clinical damage to tissue(s) and organ(s) systems.

It's worthwhile to mention here the concept of "stress antigens" that we discussed in Chapter 2, page 16. A non-substance entity like mental, emotional, physiological, or physical (injury) stress is interpreted by the immune system as "non-self" and thus, foreign" or technically, an "antigen (or immunogen)." As such, stress reduction (physical, mental, emotional, physiological, psychological) must be considered in therapies for autoimmune diseases.

PATIENT'S GENOME

Abnormalities (mutations) in the patient's genome can make it susceptible to dysregulation. A person's genes are what "predispose" them or provides the genetic susceptibility to dysregulate the immune system, which in turn yields chronic inflammation and, in effect, creates the pathological damage to cells, tissues, and organ systems synonymous with autoimmune diseases. Almost every aspect of the immune system contributes to the pathogenesis of autoimmunity. Complicated interactions between genetic variants, epigenetics (non-altered DNA modification of phenotype gene expression), and environmental factors produce a multitude of pathways that lead to autoimmune diseases.[6] (More discussion on genetics, the genome, and autoimmunity below.)

ENVIRONMENTAL FACTORS

With the exception of endogenous antigens (sometimes referred to as "autoantigens" including such things as metabolic and immune byproducts, "rogue" APCs, stress, genetic mutations, etc.), most antigens are external "non-self" substances which the body may interpret as toxic. Pollution, allergens, mechanical or physical injury or irritation, smoking, chemicals, insect bites, stings, etc., all can be considered environmental factors or toxins as discussed in Chapter 2. In combination with the inherited alleles that an individual possesses for a specific gene (the genotype), a given environmental factor can produce a "phenotype trigger" to produce the clinical manifestations of autoimmune disease.

Consider the person who has smoked all their life without ever experiencing the classic, associated diseases (respiratory, cardio-vascular, carcinogenic). One would use this as an argument that smoking is not a risk factor. On the contrary. That individual rolled the dice (unknowingly) on not having the specific gene(s) to induce smoke-related disease, and won. But epidemiologic stud-ies have unequivocally concluded that there is a greater risk of having one or more "phenotype triggers" for smoking-induced disease than not. Of course, this applies to all environmental fac-tors. But the free will choices we make regarding what we will or will not expose (risk) ourselves to range from common sense to practicing personal and public health. Indeed, the environmental factors we choose differ considerably from the ones our genes (from allergies to cancers) choose for us. Heredity patterns and DNA testing (karyotypes) tell us a great deal about these environ-mental risks.

INCREASING RELEASE AND ACCUMULATION OF PRO-INFLAMMATORY CYTOKINES

As the immune system fights off foreign antigens, it is continu-ally releasing inflammatory proteins called "pro-inflammatory cytokines." If the pathological antigen is not successfully eliminated in a timely fashion, the pro-inflammatory cytokines accumulate in the tissue in abnormal amounts and are interpreted by the adaptive immune system as antigenic (foreign) and perpetuate an autoim-mune response.

ABNORMAL IMMUNE RESPONSE TO "SELF"

Finally, autoimmune disease can simply be stated as an "abnormal immune response to 'self'." But such a simple statement is belied by the many theories that abound as to the cause and true pathogenesis of the disease category. Currently, the exact cause of autoimmune disorders is unknown. One theory is that some microorganisms (such as bacteria or viruses) or drugs may trigger changes that confuse the immune system. This may happen more often in people who have genes that make them more prone to autoimmune disorders.[7] Other possible etiologies for autoantigenicity include disruption of homeostasis (Yin Yang from Chapter 2, page 16); innate autoantigens from an inflammatory process; and "rogue" antigen-presenting cells (APCs).[8]

REVIEW OF AI FOR THE THEORIES OF AUTOIMMUNITY PATHOGENESIS

To repeat the reverse corollary to the statement made in Chapter 3, page 39, one can make a categorical statement that all AI-addressing autoimmune diseases apply to chronic inflammation as well. As such, it would be worthwhile to review both related sections on AI applications in Chapters 3 and 4 as you read these literature thumbnails.

1   Autoimmune diseases are mostly characterized by autoantibodies in the patients' serum or cerebrospinal fluid, representing diagnostic or prognostic biomarkers. Research has focused on single autoantigens or panels of single autoantigens. Unsupervised machine learning can broaden the focus by addressing the entire autoantigen repertoire in a systemic "omics-like" way. This approach aims to capture the enormous biodiversity in the sets of targeted antigens and pave the way toward a more holistic understanding of the concerted character of antibody-related humoral immune responses permitting high-throughput screenings of thousands of autoantigens in parallel. Clusters of autoantigens can be identified that share certain functional or

spatial properties, or clusters of patients comprising clinical subgroups potentially useful for patient stratification. This may enhance the understanding of autoimmune diseases in a more comprehensive way compared to current single or panel autoantibodies approaches.[9]

2 Unraveling the genetic and environmental underpinnings of autoimmune disease has become a major focus at the National Institute of Environmental Health Sciences of the National Institute of Health. The process of identifying the offending genetic sites (likely multiple mutations) in the person's genome is overwhelming. The potential for those mutations in the sequencing of the four base compounds within the 20,000–25,000 genes in the human genome exceeds 2.5×10^{20} possibilities spread among the 37.2 trillion somatic cells. Thanks to AI, more specifically, big data analytics and deep learning (convolutional neural networking – CNN), genetic loci for immune disorders (immunodeficiencies) are now being identified in a timely diagnostic manner (days to weeks versus months to years). This application of AI to better identify genetic mutations and their associated disease states combined with the new FDA-approved cellular and gene therapies (presented below), has created new horizons in the treatments, management, cures, and prevention of disease.

3 Advances in "omics" technologies (e.g., epigenomics, genomics, transcriptomics, proteomics, metabolomics, etc.), also called systems-based approach, are now utilized to identify molecular targets including biomarkers that can reveal the disease state or the ability to respond to a specific treatment, thus providing scientists and clinicians the ability to generate a machine learning data set consisting of molecular insights of the disease pathogenesis.[10]

4 Machine learning algorithms allow categorization of patients based on their specific differences through screening a patient's genome, transcriptome, proteome, epigenome, immunome, and microbiome. Integrating the omics data sets using systems biology-based approaches may advance understanding of the

underlying causative factors in individual patients. Artificial intelligence could contribute to the diagnosis and prognosis of autoimmune diseases, and whether it could assist with predictions of therapy efficacy and adverse effects. AI offers enormous potential for personalized medicine in autoimmune diseases and evaluating the feasibility of big data in disease management.[11]

5   AI technologies are starting to deliver promising results in different fields of aging and longevity research. The most important alterations of aging occur in the adaptive immune system and involve T-cells. Many of these alterations are assumed to decrease capacity of the immune system to combat an emerging or progressing tumor. The declining function of the immune system is known as immunosenescence and leads to a higher incidence of infection, cancer, and autoimmune disease-related mortalities in the elderly population.[12]

CLINICAL MANIFESTATIONS OF AUTOIMMUNE DISORDERS

VASCULAR SYSTEM

As presented in Chapter 3, the effects of chronic inflammation are profound and broadly deleterious to tissues and organ systems throughout the body. The principal reason for this diffuse pathological process is the affects chronic inflammation has on the network of blood vessels (particularly the adventitia and endothelial lining of their walls – perivasculitis) supplying all of the bodily tissues and organs. These pathological effects manifest themselves in the form of clinical entities categorized as the autoimmune diseases (Table 4.1). Whereas, the underlying cause of the disease process is in effect chronic inflammation, the clinical manifestations present themselves as specific tissue and organ system diseases (secondary to the chronic inflammation).

When considering the multiple theories of the pathogenesis of autoimmune diseases (above), it is apparent that there are in fact numerous causes (persistent antigens, environmental, autoantigens, etc.) beyond strictly the vascular component we describe. However, as posited throughout this discussion, we come back to the ultimate predicate that the adaptive immune response leads to chronic inflammation, which ultimately leads to all autoimmune diseases.

DIFFUSE ORGAN SYSTEMS

To be more specific as to the autoimmune diseases associated with tissue(s) and organ systems, I would refer you back to Table 4.1 which lists all the diseases associated with the autoimmune response. And to further emphasize the prevalent nature of autoimmune disease (approximately 8% of the general population),[13] Table 4.3 lists the top ten autoimmune diseases. I'm sure you will note the "popularity" of each of these diseases in today's world. Also noteworthy in the list (as well as the Table 4.1 listings) is that many of the diseases are organ-specific (e.g., Crohn's disease), some are tissue-specific (e.g., psoriasis), and some who's pathology is diffuse (e.g., rheumatoid arthritis, systemic lupus erythematosus).

Table 4.3 Ten (10) Most Common Autoimmune Diseases

- Rheumatoid arthritis
- Systemic lupus erythematosus (SLE)
- Inflammatory bowel disease (IBD)
- Crohn's disease
- Multiple sclerosis (MS)
- Type 1 diabetes mellitus
- Guillain-Barré syndrome
- Psoriasis
- Graves' disease
- Myasthenia gravis

Source: Foundations of AI in Healthcare and Bioscience; Catania; Academy Press. November 2020.

REVIEW OF AI FOR THE CLINICAL MANIFESTATIONS OF AUTOIMMUNE DISORDERS

1   A company has developed a wearable device (BioBeats), an app and machine learning system that collects data and monitors users' level of stress before predicting when it could be the cause of a more serious or physical health condition. It measures several vital signs, including blood pressure, stroke volume, pulse rate, pulse pressure, heart rate variability, respiratory rate, saturation, cardiac output, cardiac index, and more. The data is transmitted to BioBeat's application and is available on the individual's cellular phone, tablet, or as a full monitoring system in a hospital department. When combined with in-app mood-tracking, deep breathing exercises, and executive function tests, it can provide a comprehensive overview of one's mental and physical well-being.[14]

2   Machine learning (ML) and artificial intelligence are most commonly applied to multiple sclerosis (MS), rheumatoid arthritis (RA), and inflammatory bowel disease (IBD), generating models using two data types (always including clinical data). Random forests and support vector machines are commonly used methods throughout diseases and applications. Clinical data used in models for every type of autoimmune disease, and models using genetic data were created for the majority of disorders. The applications for ML are categorized into six broad topics: patient identification, risk prediction, diagnosis, disease subtype classification, disease progression and outcome, and monitoring and management.[15]

3   A study was conducted to determine if animal, dietary, recreational, or occupational exposures are associated with multiple sclerosis (MS) risk. The machine learning method of least absolute shrinkage and selection operator (LASSO) regression were used to identify a subset of exposures with potential relevance to disease in a large population-based, case-control study. There was a suggestive association of pesticide exposure with having MS among men, but only in those who were positive for HLA-DRB1. Machine learning approaches may be useful for future investigations of concomitant MS risk or prognostic factors.[16]

4   A study was performed to explore potential regulatory mech-
    anisms and identifying immunogenic prognostic markers for
    breast cancer (BC), which were used to construct a prognostic
    signature for disease-free survival (DFS) of BC based on arti-
    ficial intelligence algorithms. Differentially expressed immune
    genes were identified between normal tissues and tumor tis-
    sues. Comprehensive bioinformatics identified [17] immune genes
    as potential prognostic biomarkers, which might be potential
    candidates of immunotherapy targets in BC patients. The study
    depicted regulatory network between transcription factors and
    immune genes, which was helpful to deepen the understanding
    of immune regulatory mechanisms for BC.[17]

5   One of the main challenges in medical microbiology is to
    develop novel experimental approaches, which enables a better
    understanding of bacterial infections and antimicrobial resist-
    ance (especially in light of the COVID-19 pandemic). Today, the
    use of in silico experiments (research conducted by means of
    computer modeling or computer simulation) jointly with com-
    putational and machine learning offer an in-depth understand-
    ing of systems biology, allowing us to use this knowledge for
    the prevention, prediction, and control of infectious disease.
    An in-depth knowledge of host-pathogen-protein interactions,
    combined with a better understanding of a host's immune
    response and bacterial fitness, are key determinants for halting
    infectious diseases and antimicrobial resistance dissemination.[18]

AUTOIMMUNE DISEASE CATEGORIES

Throughout our discussions of specific disease entities, you will
recognize common denominators in their diagnosis and treatments
(as mentioned previously in the discussion in Chapter 3, page
43–46, on "non-specific" drug therapies in autoimmune disease).
What will change for each disorder are the clinical manifestations
(phenotypes) of the individual disease categories based on cellular,
tissue, and organ system(s) involved.[19]

DISEASE DESCRIPTIONS

A person's genes are what "predispose" them or provide genetic susceptibility to dysregulate the immune system, which in turn yields chronic inflammation and, in effect, creates the pathological damage to cells, tissues, and organ systems synonymous with autoimmune diseases. The environmental factors mentioned previously (e.g., smoking, pollution) along with the inherited alleles that an individual possesses for a specific gene (the genotype), combine to produce the "phenotype trigger" and the clinical manifestations of the disease state.

This recipe for a disease is responsible for immune and autoimmune diseases as well as congenital and acquired genetic diseases, for cancers, and in fact, for just about all disease conditions. Thus, specific autoimmune diseases include common denominators in their pathogenesis, diagnosis, and treatments (as described in the discussion on "non-specific" drug therapies in Chapter 3). What does change for each autoimmune disorder are the clinical manifestations (phenotypes) of the individual disease based on cellular, tissue, and organ system(s) involvement.[20]

This genetic approach to disease has led to the concept of "precision medicine" which aims to understand how a person's genetics, environment, and lifestyle can help determine the best approach to prevent or treat disease.[21] The National Institute of Health (NIH) has launched a study, known as the "All of Us" Research Program, which involves a group (cohort) of at least one million volunteers from around the United States. Participants are providing genetic data, biological samples, and other information about their health.[22] The long-term goals are to bringing precision medicine to all areas of health care on a large scale.

REVIEW OF AI FOR AUTOIMMUNE DISEASE CATEGORIES

Listed below are the top ten autoimmune diseases (from Table 4.3) and an example (from among many) of recent AI applications and influence for each condition.

1 Rheumatoid arthritis (RA): A recent study in JAMA Network Open shows that AI models can use electronic health record data

to prognosticate future patient outcomes in RA. A longitudinal deep learning model was used to predict disease activity for 820 patients with RA at their next rheumatology clinic visit and was compared to last disease activity for predictive value. The longitudinal deep learning model had strong performance, whereas baselines that used each patient's most recent disease activity score had statistically random performance.[23]

2 Systemic lupus erythematosus (SLE): Machine learning approaches were employed to integrate gene expression data from three SLEdata sets and used it to classify patients as having active or inactive disease as characterized by standard clinical composite outcome measures. Both raw whole blood gene expression data and informative gene modules were employed with various classification algorithms. The use of gene modules rather than raw gene expression was more robust, achieving classification accuracies of approximately 70% regardless of how the training and testing sets were formed.[24]

3 Inflammatory bowel disease (IBD): Following the use of immunosuppressants and biological agents, the incidence of surgery for IBD decreased. However, it is still significantly important to determine the predictors for surgery. A study enrolled 239 Crohn's Disease patients and constructed some algorithms using the patients' clinical manifestations, radiologic findings, and laboratory tests using several machine learning methods and artificial neural networks (ANNs). The Random Forest model had the highest accuracy of 96.26%.[25]

4 Crohn's disease (CD): Studies were performed using wireless capsule endoscopy in the evaluation of the gut ulcerative lesions of CD patients using support vector machine (SVM) or convolutional network. The accuracy of these algorithm models were all relatively high with rates ranging from 89.3% to 93.8%.[26]

5 Multiple sclerosis (MS): An algorithm was created that combines multiple machine-learning techniques to predict the expanded disability status scale (EDSS) score of patients with multiple sclerosis at two years solely based on age, sex, and fluid attenuated

inversion recovery (FLAIR) MRI data. The algorithm combined several complementary predictors: a pure deep learning predictor based on a convolutional neural network (CNN) that learns from the images, as well as classical machine-learning predictors. The method predicted two-year clinical disability in patients with multiple sclerosis with a mean EDSS score error of 1.7. This supports the use of this model to predict EDSS score progression.[27]

6 Type 1 diabetes: An algorithm that provides weekly insulin dosage recommendations to adults employs a unique virtual platform[28] to generate over 50,000 glucose observations to train a k-nearest neighbors decision support system (KNN-DSS) to identify causes of hyperglycemia or hypoglycemia and determine necessary insulin adjustments from a set of 12 potential recommendations. The KNN-DSS algorithm achieves an overall agreement with board-certified endocrinologists of 67.9%. Data indicate that the KNN-DSS allows for early identification of dangerous insulin regimens and may be used to improve glycemic outcomes and prevent life-threatening complications in people with T1D.[29]

7 Guillain-Barré syndrome (GBS): GBS includes acute motor axonal neuropathy, acute motor and sensory axonal neuropathy, and pharyngeal-cervical-brachial weakness. Newly developed technologies, including metabolite analysis, peripheral nerve ultrasound, and feature selection via AI are facilitating more accurate diagnosis of axonal GBS. Nevertheless, some key issues, such as genetic susceptibilities, remain unanswered and moreover, current therapies bear limitations.[30]

8 Psoriasis: Several original research articles exist on improving psoriasis classification methods using AI applications using image recognition. One study[31] compared the ability of several applications at classifying the severity of psoriasis lesions. The systems described achieved average sensitivities between 93.81% and 99.76% and average specificities between 97% and 99.99%.

9 Graves' disease: In an effort to apply AI to the challenging task of classifying thyroid nodules, an image similarity algorithm shows accuracy that is similar, and in some aspects better, than the

best-available ultrasound-based classification systems. By using image similarity AI models, subjectivity is eliminated resulting in a decrease in the number of unnecessary biopsies, "by as much as 50%". A deep learning model was used to process all available images for 482 nodules from patients who underwent a biopsy or thyroid surgery. Overall, 66 nodules were malignant in the training set and 33 were malignant in the test nodules. The results showed the AI system had a sensitivity and specificity of 87.8% and 78.5%, respectively. Overall, the system's accuracy was 81.5%. "The results suggest the use of the image similarity AI system could result in a 57.3% reduction in biopsies."[32]

10 Myasthenia gravis (MG): Machine learning algorithms (convolutional neural networks [CNN]) were trained on 22 co-factors/features commonly found with MG, and could also predict the probability of being afflicted with MG given a patient history and a questionnaire. The goal was to eliminate the need for a painful and expensive Single-Fiber Electromyography (EMG) test and could potentially diagnose with a single anti-acetylcholine receptor (AChR) antibody (Ab) test. The CNN model performed very well since it has the highest F1 (accuracy) score among all the other models. The model allowed for picking the features that strongly control the prediction since it used a convolution and max pooling layer.[33]

DIAGNOSIS OF AUTOIMMUNE DISEASE

The diagnosis of autoimmune disease can be challenging for two reasons. First, many of the associated diseases share similar symptoms. Second, as described previously, the disease process may be organ-specific or disseminated among multiple body systems. The diagnostic evaluation includes a thorough history, physical examination, laboratory testing, and imaging based on suspected tissue or organ-system involvement(s). Any additional tests mentioned in the diagnosis of chronic inflammation in Chapter 3 (page 41) should be considered part of an autoimmune disease evaluation as well.

PHYSICAL EXAMINATION

In autoimmune disease, signs and symptoms can vary considerably. As opposed to acute inflammation, chronic inflammation in autoimmune diseases can be difficult to identify without a history of precipitating acute inflammation. A chronically ill patient can be assumed to have chronic inflammation. (This was mentioned previously, that "…chronic inflammatory disease is the progenitor or originating cause of *all* the major human disease categories.")[34,35]

A listing of the non-specific symptoms most associated with autoimmune disease include[36]

- fatigue;
- achy muscles;
- swelling and redness;
- low-grade fever;
- trouble concentrating;
- numbness and tingling in the hands and feet;
- hair loss;
- skin rashes.
- body pain;
- fever (often diagnostically referred to as "fever of unknown origin" or FUO;
- constant fatigue and insomnia;
- depression, anxiety and mood disorders;
- gastrointestinal complications like constipation, diarrhea, and acid reflux;
- weight gain;
- frequent infections.

In the case of immunosuppression or immunocompromised disease conditions, the symptoms are usually indirect as in increased illnesses, risk of infection, blood disorders, digestive problems, and delayed growth and development.[37] Regarding the array of autoimmune diseases, there are more than 80 identified affecting more than 50 million Americans (according to the American Auto-immune Disease Related Association, AARDA), of whom 75% are women.[38] Table 4.1 listed the more prevalent autoimmune diseases, and Table 4.3 identified the top 10, which are undoubtedly quite familiar to most. Relative to the specific conditions, symptoms range from no symptoms at all to general malaise to severe illness and risk of death (as is the case for many COVID-19 patients, particularly with obesity).[39]

LABORATORY

No single laboratory test can diagnose autoimmune diseases. It requires a physical examination to assess signs and symptoms with a combination of lab tests. The antinuclear antibody test (ANA) is often one of the first tests used when symptoms suggest an autoimmune disease. A positive ANA test suggests the potential presence of auto-immune disease, but it does not confirm exactly which one or even if one is present for certain. Other tests look for specific autoantibodies produced in certain autoimmune diseases. The bottom line is laboratory diagnosis is non-specific and can only assist in the symptoms and other tests to confirm the diagnosis.[40]

IMAGING

Based on a tentative diagnosis of an autoimmune disease, there is a likelihood that tissue(s) and organ(s) associated with the specific disease will demonstrate identifiable pathology. Autoimmune respiratory diseases will show distinct changes in lung x-rays; gastrointestinal-related diseases will demonstrate distinct changes in endoscopic examinations; multiple sclerosis will reveal certain cerebral changes (e.g., calcifications on MRI scans). The combination of positive laboratory and imaging diagnostic indicators are all contributory, but only in combination with a careful physical assessment and patient history.

REVIEW OF AI IN THE DIAGNOSIS OF AUTOIMMUNE DISEASE

1   In one year in the United States it was reported that 31% of medical lawsuits were related to either an inordinate delay in the diagnosis or failure to make the correct diagnosis. It is anticipated that precision medicine (PM) coupled with artificial intelligence (AI), machine learning (ML), and deep neural networks (DNN) will help health care providers stay abreast of current literature, predict individual susceptibility to primary or secondary autoinflammatory and autoimmune conditions.[41]

2   Researcher used the ImmunoChip data set containing 18,227 Crohn's Disease patients and 34,050 healthy controls enrolled and genotyped by the International Inflammatory Bowel Disease Genetics Consortium to be re-analyzed via a set of machine learning methods. They managed to detect nearly all the genetic variants previously identified by human genome-wide association studies (GWAS) among the best predictors, plus additional predictors with lower effects. Overall, such an approach may provide a more superior alternative method to traditional experimental colitis method of understanding the disease by allowing analysis of complex systems through crunching of big data.[42]

3   The application of precision immunoprofiling by image analysis and artificial intelligence to biology and disease was demonstrated in a study where immunoprofiling data was used to assess immuno-oncology biomarkers, such as PD-L1 checkpoint inhibitors and immune cell infiltrates as predictors of patient's response to cancer treatment.[43]

4   Identification of patients with autoimmune diseases was studied utilizing machine learning (ML) methods and employing natural language processing (NLP) methods from electronic medical records. The algorithms were intended to replace International Classification of Diseases billing codes, which have error rates of between 17.1% and 76.9% due to inconsistent terminology. The AI process improved the efficiency of algorithms for this

purpose. Prediction of disease risk and identification of novel risk factors through feature selection was documented for IBD, type 1 diabetes (T1D), RA, systemic lupus erythematosus (SLE) and MS. ML, specifically for early diagnosis was specified by seven studies for the later onset degenerative conditions MS and RA. Disease progression and outcome was a focus for 27 studies. Other considered issues were disease severity; treatment response; and survival prediction. Disease progression and outcome were the second-most prevalent areas for model development. The most common models were support vector machines, random forest, and neural networks. The majority of data used was clinical, with very few papers utilizing 'omic data. These models could be applied to more difficult tasks that reflect the complexity of autoimmune disease. With these advances, AI and ML have the potential to bring personalized medicine closer for patients with complex and chronic disease.[44]

5   For the first time, scientists at the Human Vaccines Project are combining systems biology with artificial intelligence to understand one of the most significant remaining frontiers of human health, the human immune system.[45] Perhaps the most exciting application of AI in immunology is found in the Human Vaccines Project. Researchers are comprehensively sequencing the human immune system, a system billions of times larger than the human genome. The goal is to encode the genes responsible for circulating B-cell receptors. This can provide potential new antibody targets for vaccines and therapeutics that work across populations. The Project seeks to define the genetic underpinnings of people's ability to respond and adapt to an immense range of diseases.[46]

The SARS-CoV-2 COVID-19 pandemic will certainly expedite further progress on this critical area of clinical research. The study specifically looked at one part of the adaptive immune system, the circulating B-cell receptors that are responsible for the production of antibodies, considered the primary determinant of immunity in people. The receptors form unique sequences of nucleotides known as receptor "clonotypes." This creates a small number of genes that can lead to an incredible diversity of receptors, allowing the immune system to recognize almost any new pathogen.

This project marks a crucial step toward understanding how the human immune system works, setting the stage for developing next-generation health products, drugs, and vaccines through the convergence of genomics and immune monitoring technologies with machine learning and artificial intelligence.[47]

TREATMENT OF AUTOIMMUNE DISEASES

MEDICAL THERAPIES

Chronic inflammation and autoimmune diseases often require treatment directed at the tissue(s) and organ system(s) being adversely affected. Some of those organ-specific treatments are used in conditions related directly and indirectly as well to cancers, type 1 diabetes, and many other autoimmune diseases. More generalized treatment falls under the category of immunosuppressive and immunomodulating (suppressing or stimulating) therapies, sometimes referred to as "non-specific therapies" (discussed in Chapter 3, page 43–46). These therapies include types of drugs that are used to suppress immune system auto-antigenicity in autoimmune diseases or to boost the immune system response in cancers and anti-tumor therapies. Immunization and vaccine approaches can also be considered medical, immunotherapies for autoimmune diseases and are discussed in Chapters 3 and 5.

THERAPEUTIC PROCEDURES

Autoimmune disease, like its progenitor chronic inflammation, may be organ-specific in its cellular damage (e.g., Crohn's disease, Graves' disease, etc.), or its harm may be disseminated in multiple organ systems throughout the body (e.g., systemic lupus erythematosus, giant-cell arteritis, rheumatoid arthritis). Thus, treatments for autoimmune disease beyond the drug classes mentioned above must be targeted, organ-specific therapies, or treatments disseminated throughout the body via cellular and genetic pathways. This is also the case in cancer therapies. Thus, multiple treatment options and approaches are common to both autoimmune diseases and cancers (effectively an autoimmune disease itself). Among the treatment options common to autoimmune diseases and cancers, besides the drug categories mentioned above, genetic methodologies and cell transplantation therapies have become viable methods of treatment.

STEM CELL TRANSPLANTATION (REGENERATIVE MEDICINE)

Transplantation procedures include a number of methods of delivery of a targeted therapeutic gene including direct delivery and cell delivery (Figure 4.1). Direct delivery packages the gene into a vehicle such as a genetically engineered retrovirus which is injected into the patient, whereupon it penetrates the genome and thus, is delivered to the targeted organ system. The weakness to this method of delivery includes the random integration of the gene into the patient's chromosomes with unknown, potential adverse effects. The stem cell delivery method removes cells from the patient and introduces the "packaged gene" in the cells (in vitro) and returns them back into the patient. The use of undifferentiated embryonic stem (ES) cells as the vehicle for gene re-transplantation to the patient (autologous transplantation) offers additional specificity to the process where the ES cells can replicate only in the target organ.[48]

Stem cell transplantation and immunogenomic (CRISPR-Cas9 and CAR-T cell, below) therapies have been well received in immunologic and immunogenic therapies. They are rapidly approaching the standard of care for targeted, organ-specific treatments as well as disseminated and genomic therapies. Effectively, stem cell transplantation,

Stem cell transplantation and CAR-T cell (gene) replacement

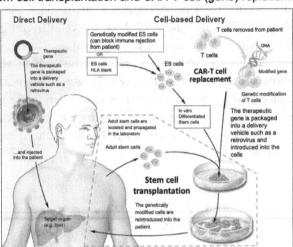

Figure 4.1 Stem cell transplantation and CAR-T-cell (gene) replacement. (National Institute of Health, U.S. Dept. of Health and Human Services.)

CAR-T cell replacement therapy, gene replacement therapies, and CRISPR-Cas9 (gene editing) have similar applications, albeit with different therapeutic goals in autoimmune diseases, genetic disorders, cancers, and numerous other congenital, acquired, and chronic conditions. It is important to note here that these innovative and "disruptive" biomedical and cellular therapies for autoimmune diseases enjoy the benefits that piggyback on the successes of genetic and cancer treatments and vis a versa.[49]

Hematopoietic stem cell therapy (a "blood stem cell" that can develop into all types of blood cells found in the peripheral blood, the bone marrow, and immune cells)[50] is now being used effectively (regenerative medicine) to grow new cellular and immunological based strategies for patients with malignancy and hematological disorders produced or provoked by immunologic or autoimmunologic causes. Stem cells can be readily harvested from bone marrow and adipose tissue (and other bodily tissues) and converted into undifferentiated induced pluripotent cells (iPSC – reprogrammed embryonic-like cells capable of developing into any type of human cell, a 2012 Nobel Prize award winning technology) suitable for transplantation into diseased and degenerated organs and body structures (e.g., diabetes, osteoarthritis, etc.). These cells then regenerate and begin to replace the abnormal cells with new, normal cells including immune system cells, and even potentially with functioning organs (organ morphogenesis).[51] (Figure 4.2) Currently, muscle and bone tissue are particularly responsive to stem cell regeneration.

All medical treatments have benefits and risks, but unproven stem cell therapies can be particularly unsafe. The FDA will continue to help with the development and licensing of new stem cell therapies where the scientific evidence supports the product's safety and effectiveness.[52]

Stem Cell Self Renewal and Differentiation

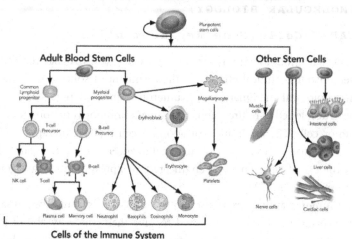

Figure 4.2 Stem cell renewal and differentiation. (Maharaj Institute of Immune Regenerative Medicine.)

The objective of stem cell transplantation therapy is to destroy the mature, long-lived, and auto-reactive immune cells and generate a new, properly functioning immune system. The patient's stem cells are used in a procedure known as autologous (from "one's self") hematopoietic stem cell transplantation (Figure 4.1). First, patients receive injections of a growth factor, which coaxes large numbers of hematopoietic stem cells to be released from the bone marrow into the bloodstream. These cells are harvested from the blood, purified away from mature immune cells, and stored. After sufficient quantities of these cells are obtained, the patient undergoes a regimen of cytotoxic (cell-killing) drug and/or radiation therapy, which eliminates the mature immune cells. Then, the hematopoietic stem cells are returned to the patient via a blood transfusion into the circulation where they migrate to the bone marrow and begin to differentiate to become mature immune cells. The body's immune system is then restored.[53]

IMMUNOGENETICS AND IMMUNOGENOMICS (MOLECULAR BIOLOGY)

CAR-T Cell (Gene Replacement)

Cancer immunotherapy is a rapidly growing field that has recently demonstrated clinical efficacy in the treatment of solid tumors and hematological malignancies.[54] Numerous clinical approaches have been developed to redirect and/or augment immune function against tumor cells. The application of adoptive cell transfer therapy (ACT therapy) for the treatment of malignant cancers has been expanded by the use of T lymphocytes engineered to express chimeric antigen receptors (CARs).[55]

Chimeric antigen receptor T-cells (CAR-T-cells) are T-cells that have been genetically engineered to give them the new ability to target a specific protein. The receptors are "chimeric" because they combine both antigen-binding and T-cell activating functions into a single receptor. The premise of CAR-T immunotherapy is to modify T-cells to recognize cancer cells to more effectively target and destroy them.[56] CAR-T-cell therapy (see Figure 4.1) begins by removing a patient's T lymphocytes and transducing them with a DNA plasmid vector (a DNA molecule distinct from the cell's DNA used as a tool to clone, transfer, and manipulate genes)[57] that encodes specific tumor antigens. These modified and targeted lymphocytes are then reintroduced to the patient's body through a single infusion to attack tumor cells. Known as autologous CAR-T-cell therapy, this treatment has been in development for more than 25 years, resulting in four generations of improving therapy that has generated responses for up to four years in some studies.[58]

There are currently two FDA-approved CAR-T products used in cell malignancies.[59] Based upon the high rates of initial cancer remission and durable responses in many patients receiving CAR-T-cell therapy, the ACT field has expanded with CAR-T-cell therapy now being applied against numerous other B-cell-associated antigens with encouraging clinical response data being reported.[60] Again, as previously described above, about the combination of stem cells with CRISPR-Cas9, so too can CAR-T-cell therapies be expanded in such combinations. To increase the efficiency of the CAR-T-cells, CRISPR-Cas9 has been used to increase their antitumor efficiency by disrupting a programmed death protein.[61]

CRISPR-Cas9 (Gene Editing)

One of the effective ways of treating autoimmune disease is to identify the "signature" of offending genes (their "gene expression" or the number of RNA molecules they are producing), which is abnormal in autoimmune (and cancer) genes. This identification is accomplished using a technique called 'single-cell RNA sequencing' (scRNA-seq), or more specifically, TIDE (for Tumor Immune Dysfunction and Exclusion) for autoimmune genes.[62] With this information, a procedure called CRISPR-Cas9 (Clustered regularly interspaced short palindromic repeats-associated protein 9), an RNA-guided genome editing technology, is being used to re-engineer T-cells.

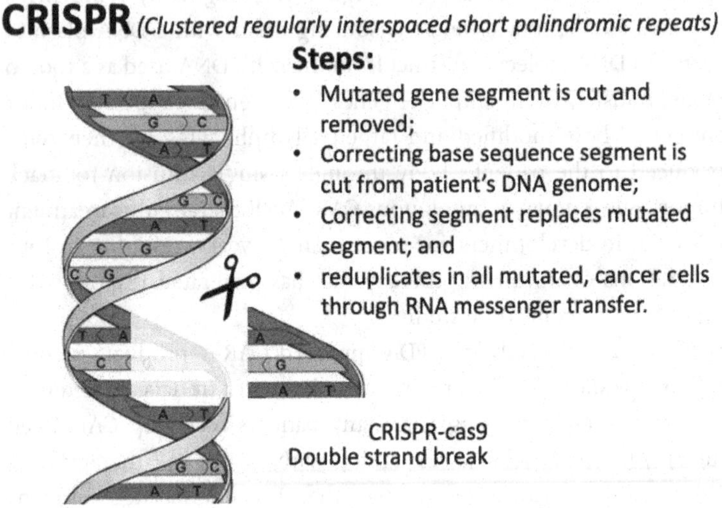

CRISPR (Clustered regularly interspaced short palindromic repeats)

Steps:

- Mutated gene segment is cut and removed;
- Correcting base sequence segment is cut from patient's DNA genome;
- Correcting segment replaces mutated segment; and
- reduplicates in all mutated, cancer cells through RNA messenger transfer.

CRISPR-cas9
Double strand break

Figure 4.3 CRISPR-Cas9. (Louis J. Catania ©1996.)

The CRISPR-Cas9 system (Figure 4.3)[63] creates a small piece of RNA with a short "guide" sequence that attaches (binds) to a specific target sequence of DNA identified by AI in a genome. The RNA also binds to the Cas9 enzyme and is used to recognize the DNA sequence. The Cas9 enzyme acting as a "scissor" cuts the DNA at the targeted location. Once the DNA is cut, the cell's DNA uses its repair machinery to add or delete pieces of genetic material, or to make changes to the DNA by replacing an existing segment with a customized DNA sequence.[64]

It was first thought that the stitching back together of the genetic material after the CRISPR-Cas9 procedure was random.[65] But subsequent studies using a trained machine learning algorithm called inDelphi to predict repairs made to DNA snipped with Cas9, used guide RNAs to induce a single, predictable repair genotype in the human genome in more than 50% of editing products (see AI Review #2 below). This study proved that the edits aren't random.

It is worth noting here that the 2020 Nobel Prize in Chemistry was awarded to 2 molecular biologists, Emmanuelle Charpentier of the Max Planck Unit for the Science of Pathogens Institute for Infection Biology and Jennifer Doudna of the University of California, Berkeley, for the development of this revolutionary genome editing technique often referred to as "genetic scissors." (Footnote: Press Release: The Nobel Prize in Chemistry 2020. The Royal Swedish Academy of Sciences. 7 October 2020). Further explanation of this CRISPR procedure, RNA sequencing, and the AI applications that make it possible can be found in Chapter 5, "CRISPR-Cas13 and RNA Screening," page 112.

Also worth noting here is the costs of CAR-T and CRISPR-Cas9 therapy as well as the other immunotherapies discussed. Notwithstanding the significant benefits of these therapies provide, the costs are exorbitant. FDA-approved CAR-T-cell therapy and the CRISPR-Cas9 procedure range from \$373,000 to \$875,000 for a single treatment.[68] Depending on the type of stem cell procedure, prices can range from \$5,000 to \$25,000 per procedure.[69]

Gene therapies are subject not only to the regulatory structure of the FDA, but also to the Office of Biotechnology Activities, and the Recombinant DNA Advisory Committee. Excessive regulatory oversight creates an elongated and expensive route to approval. Gene therapies provide those with rare, serious, and possibly terminal conditions with the ability to improve their quality of life significantly. By one estimate, approval for a gene therapy costs nearly \$5 billion (five times as high as the average cost of FDA drug approvals).[70] Some insurers are beginning partial coverage of FDA-approved gene therapies, but experimental treatments receive no third-party coverage other than limited humanitarian exemptions.

The role of immunology in both our personnel health and welfare and the public health comes front and center as we review acute inflammation, chronic inflammation, and autoimmune disease, and their AI-supported treatment options as discussed in Chapters 2–4. Reinforcing the immunologic options from the basic removal of the antigenic cause through the sophistication of immunotherapies and immunogenic procedures, we can consider immunology as "the center of the therapeutic health care universe." That role and its enigmatic paradox of the immune system being our "best friend" and "worst enemy" is now providential as the world faces its most existential threat in the COVID-19 pandemic. In Chapter 5, we will address the "best" and the "worst" of that challenge and AI and immunology's critical role in attacking the SARS-CoV-2 virus.

REVIEW OF AI IN THE TREATMENT FOR AUTOIMMUNE DISEASES

1   AI can be used to identify the state of development of embryonic cells. Embryonic AI is an ensemble of DNNs trained and validated on transcriptomics data representative of healthy ESC, iPSC, EPC, ASC, and AC types. Using data provided by the user, the system will output an embryonic score.[71]

2   A study reported in *Nature* showed that template-free Cas9 editing is predictable and capable of precise repair to a predicted genotype, enabling correction of disease-associated mutations in humans. A machine learning algorithm called inDelphi was used to predict repairs made to DNA snipped with Cas9 using experimental data from 1,8[72] target sequences cut and then restitched in mouse and human cell lines. inDelphi predicts that 5%–11% of Cas9 guide RNAs targeting the human genome are 'precise-50', yielding a single genotype comprising greater than or equal to 50% of all major editing products. Based on a library of 41,630 guide RNAs and the sequences of the targeted loci before and after repair – a data set that totaled more than one billion repairs in various cell types.[66] The algorithm was then able to use the sequences that determine each repair to predict Cas9 editing outcomes.[67] The study establishes an approach for precise, template-free genome editing.[72]

3   Macrophage cells resist artificial receptors (viral, etc.) and thus, prepare them for cancer immunotherapy applications. Researchers at the University of Pennsylvania not only incorporated

chimeric antigen receptors (CARs) with macrophages, they also unleashed their newly acquired firepower to kill tumors in human samples in the lab as well as in humanized mouse models. According to the researchers, their genetically modified macrophages – CAR macrophages – may prove to be especially useful in attacking solid tumors, which often leave CAR-T-cells exhausted and defeated. Macrophages eat invading cells rather than targeting them for destruction the way T-cells do.[73]

4   AI algorithms have been developed to predict patient responses to treatment with stem cells and engineered products. AI is being used to model potential outcomes and to model complex tissue engineering methods. Fabrication of different models can also be done using robots with batch-to-batch consistency maintained. AI can be very useful in modeling potential outcomes of culturing different cells together, in a way helping to delineate how organs are formed. It can predict the outcomes of complex experiments being developed and it will aid in understanding organ formation in vivo.[74]

5   Several agents have been shown to induce and increase the immune response in many cancers. Checkpoint inhibitors have revolutionized cancer treatment and their success is mainly due to a durable immune response in cancer. The immune response is patient-specific and thus requires patient-specific treatment. AI can be utilized to predict patient responses and to come up with the right amount of inhibitors to be used. The presence of different immune cells makes the prediction difficult. Scientists have started developing algorithms that can predict immune cell population responses to different inhibitors and how the patient will respond.[75]

NOTES

1   Orbai AM. Autoimmune disease: Why is my immune system attacking itself? *Johns Hopkins Health*. 2019.

2   Kuchroo VK, Ohashi PS, Sartor RB, et al. Dysregulation of immune homeostasis in autoimmune diseases. *Nat. Med.* 2012;18:42–47.

3   Fairweather D. Rose NR. Women and autoimmune diseases. *Emerg Infect Dis.* November 2004;10(11):2005–2011.

4   Larson C. New theories explaining why women are more susceptible to autoimmune disease than men. *Managed Healthcare*. June 10, 2020.

5   Disease Development. How do autoimmune diseases unfold? *Johns Hopkins Medicine Pathology*. 2019.

6   Tsokos GC. Autoimmunity and organ damage in systemic lupus erythematosus. *Nat Immunol*. 2020;21:605–614. doi: 10.1038/s41590-020-0677-6.

7   Medline. Autoimmune disorders. U.S. National library of medicine. U.S. Department of health and human services. *National Institutes of Health*. July 2, 2020.

8   Kelly PN. Cells gone rogue. *Science*. March 13, 2020;367(6483):1208.

9   Moritzae CP, Paul S, Stoevesan O, et al. Autoantigenomics: Holistic characterization of autoantigen repertoires for a better understanding of autoimmune diseases. *Autoimmun Rev*. February 2020;19(2):102450.

10 Seyhan AA, Carini C. Are innovation and new technologies in precision medicine paving a new era in patients centric care? *J Transl Med*. 2019;17(1):114. Published 2019 April 5. doi: 10.1186/s12967-019-1864-9.

11 Seyed NS, Madgwick M, Sudhakar P, et al. Big data in IBD: Big progress for clinical practice. *BMJ*. 69(8). http://orcid.org/0000-0001-9612-0012.

12 Pawelec G. Age and immunity: What is "immunosenescence"? *Exp. Gerontol*. 2018;105:4–9.

13 Hayterab SM, Cookac MC. Updated assessment of the prevalence, spectrum and case definition of autoimmune disease. *Autoimmun Rev*. August 2012;11(10):754–765.

14 Fearn N. Can artificial intelligence help prevent mental illness? *Forbes*. September 3, 2019.

15 Stafford IS, Kellermann M, Mossotto E, Beattie RM, MacArthur BD, Ennis S. A systematic review of the applications of artificial intelligence and machine learning in autoimmune diseases. *NPJ Digit Med*. 2020;3:30. Published 2020 March 9. doi: 10.1038/s41746-020-0229-3.

16 Mowry EM, Hedström AK, Gianfrancesco MA, et al. Incorporating machine learning approaches to assess putative environmental risk factors for multiple sclerosis. *Mult Scler Relat Disord*. August 2018;24:135–141.

17 Zhang Z, Li J, He T, et al. Bioinformatics identified 17 immune genes as prognostic biomarkers for breast cancer: Application study based on artificial intelligence algorithms. *Front. Oncol*. March 31, 2020. doi: 10.3389/fonc.2020.00330.

18 Cartelle Gestal M, Dedloff MR, Torres-Sangiao E. Computational health engineering applied to model infectious diseases and antimicrobial resistance spread. Appl. Sci. June 18, 2019;9(12):2486. doi: 10.3390/app 9122486.

19 Campbell M. Genotype vs. Phenotype: Examples and definitions. *Genomic Research*. April 18, 2019.

20 Ibid. Campbell. 19.

21 Genetics Home Reference. What is the difference between precision medicine and personalized medicine? NIH. *National U.S. Library of Medicine*. USA.gov. October 15, 2019.

22 Genetics Home Reference. What is the precision medicine initiative? NIH. *National U.S. Library of Medicine*. USA.gov. October 15, 2019.

23 Cush J. Artificial intelligence to predict rheumatoid disease activity. *Rheum-Now*. March 25, 2019.

24 Kegerreis B, Catalina MD, Bachali, P, et al. Machine learning approaches to predict lupus disease activity from gene expression data. *Sci Rep*. 2019;9:9617. doi: 10.1038/s41598-019-45989-0.

25 Dong Y, Xu L, Fan Y, et al. A novel surgical predictive model for Chinese Crohn's disease patients. *Medicine (Baltimore)*. November 2019;98(46):e17510.

26 Aoki T, Yamada A, Aoyama K, et al. Automatic detection of erosions and ulcerations in wireless capsule endoscopy images based on a deep convolutional neural network. *Gastrointest Endosc*. February 2019;89(2):357–363.e2.

27 Roca P, Attye A, Colas L, et al. Artificial intelligence to predict clinical disability in patients with multiple sclerosis using FLAIR MRI. *Diagn Interv Imaging*. July 7, 2020. doi: 10.1016/j.diii.2020.05.009.

28 Resalat N, El Youssef J, Tyler N, Castle J, Jacobs PG. A statistical virtual patient population for the glucoregulatory system in type 1 diabetes with integrated exercise model. *PLoS one*. 2019;14:e0217301.

29 Tyler NS, Mosquera-Lopez CM, Wilson LM, et al. An artificial intelligence decision support system for the management of type 1 diabetes. *Nat Metab*. 2020:2:612–619. doi: 10.1038/s42255-020-0212-y.

30 Shang P, Zhu M, Wang Y, et al. Axonal variants of Guillain-Barré syndrome: An update. J *Neurol*. March 5, 2020. doi: 10.1007/s00415-020-09742-2.

31 Shrivastava VK, Londhe ND, Sonawane RS, et al. A novel and robust Bayesian approach for segmentation of psoriasis lesions and its risk stratification. *Comput Methods Programs Biomed*. October 2017;150:9–22.

32 Melville NA. AI Thyroid nodule classification could reduce biopsies by 50%. *Medscape Medical News > Conference News.* November 7, 2019.

33 Tapadar A, George A. Painless prognosis of myasthenia gravis using machine learning. *Stanford Edu Report.* December 13 2018.

34 Han S. World Health Organization (WHO) ranks chronic diseases as the greatest threat to human health. *HealthLine.* July 27, 2018.

35 Chen L, Deng H, Cui H, et al. Inflammatory responses and inflammation-associated diseases in organs. *Oncotarget.* January 23; 2018;9(6): 7204–7218. doi: 10.18632/oncotarget.23208

36 Autoimmune diseases: Types, symptoms, causes, and more. *HealthLine.* 2019.

37 Primary immunodeficiency. *Mayo Clinic.* 2019.

38 Eustice C. Autoimmune disease types and treatment. *VeryWellHealth.* May 6, 2019.

39 Finer N, Garnett SP, Bruun JM. COVID-19 and obesity. *Clin Obes.* April 27, 2020;10(3):e12365. doi: 10.1111/cob.12365.

40 Sampson S. Watson S. Autoimmune diseases: Types, symptoms, causes, and more. *Healthline.* March 26, 2019.

41 Pinal-Fernandez I, Mammen AL. On using machine learning algorithms to define clinically meaningful patient subgroups. *Ann Rheum Dis.* June 21, 2019. doi: 10.1136/annrheumdis-2019-215852.

42 Romagnoni A, Jégou S, Van Steen K, et al. Comparative performances of machine learning methods for classifying Crohn Disease patients using genome-wide genotyping data. International Inflammatory Bowel Disease Genetics Consortium (IIBDGC). *Sci Rep.* July 17, 2019;9(1):10351.

43 Koelzer VH, Sirinukunwattana K, Rittscher J, et al. Precision immuno-profiling by image analysis and artificial intelligence. *Virchows Arch.* 2019;474:511–522. doi: 10.1007/s00428-018-2485-z.

44 Ibid. Stafford. 15.

45 Garrett L. Pioneering a new era in human health. *Human Vaccines Project.* 2019.

46 Soto C, Bombardi RG, Branchizio A, et al. High frequency of shared clo-notypes in human B cell receptor repertoires. Nature. February 13, 2019;566:398–402.

47 Press Release. Decoding the human immune system. *Human Vaccines Project.* February 13, 2019.

48 Zwaka TP. Use of genetically modified stem cells in experimental gene therapies. National institutes of health. *U.S. Department of Health and Human Services.* August 10, 2020.

49 Immunotherapies for autoimmune diseases. *Nat Biomed Eng.* April 5, 2019;3:247.

50 National Cancer Institute. Dictionary. *National Institute of Health.* 2019.

51 Eguizabal C, Aran B, Geens M, et al. Two decades of embryonic stem cells: A historical overview. *Hum Reprod.* 2019:1–17. doi: 10.1093/hropen/hoy024.

52 FDA warns about stem cell therapies. *U.S. Food and Drug Administration.* September 3, 2019.

53 NIH. STEM CELL INFORMATION. Autoimmune diseases and the promise of stem cell-based. National institutes of health, *U.S. Department of Health and Human Services.* August 10, 2020.

54 June CH, O'Connor RS, Kawalekar OU, et al. CAR-T cell immunotherapy for human cancer. *Science.* 2018;359:1361–1365. doi: 10.1126/science. aar6711.

55 Gill S, June CH. Going viral: Chimeric antigen receptor T-cell therapy for hematological malignancies. *Immunol Rev.* 2015;263:68–89. doi: 10.1111/imr.12243.

56 Minutolo NG, Hollander EE, Powell Jr DJ. The emergence of universal immune receptor T cell therapy for cancer. *Front. Oncol.* March 26, 2019.

57 Wikipedia. *Plasmids.* September 23, 2019.

58 Shank BR, Do B, Sevin A, et al. Chimeric antigen receptor T cells in hematologic malignancies. *Pharmacotherapy.* 2017;37(3):334–345.

59 Porter DL, Hwang W-T, Frey NV, et al. Chimeric antigen receptor T cells persist and induce sustained remissions in relapsed refractory chronic lymphocytic leukemia. *Sci Transl Med.* 2015:7:303ra139. doi: 10.1126/scitranslmed.aac5415.

60 Fry TJ, Shah NN, Orentas RJ, et al. CD22-targeted CAR-T cells induce remission in B-ALL that is naive or resistant to CD19-targeted CAR immunotherapy. *Nat Med.* 2017;24:20. doi: 10.1038/nm.4441.

61 Rupp LJ, Schumann K, Roybal KT, et al. CRISPR/Cas9-mediated PD-1 disruption enhances anti-tumor efficacy of human chimeric antigen receptor T cells. *Sci Rep.* 2017;7(1):737.

62 Benhenda M. How to better predict cancer immunotherapy results. *Medium AI Lab.* May 22, 2019.

63 Ibid. Allen. 32.

64 Genetics Home Reference. What are genome editing and CRISPR-Cas9? NIH. *National U.S. Library of Medicine.* USA.gov. October 1, 2019.

65 van Overbeek M, Capurso D, Carter MM, et al. DNA repair profiling reveals nonrandom outcomes at Cas9-mediated breaks. *Mol Cell.* August 18, 2016;63(4):633–646.

66 Shen MW, Sherwood R, et al. Predictable and precise template-free CRISPR editing of pathogenic variants. *Nature.* 2018;563:646–651.

67 Allen F, Parts L, et al. Predicting the mutations generated by repair of Cas9-induced double-strand breaks. *Nat Biotechnol.* 2019:37:64–72.

68 March RJ. Why this new gene therapy drug costs $2.1 million 2019. *Foundation for Economic Education.* June 3, 2019.

69 Hildreth C. Cost of stem cell therapy and why it's so expensive. *BioInformant.* November 21, 2018.

70 Ramina G. Regulation and oversight of gene therapy in the US. *Regulatory Focus.org.* February 2017.

71 Zhavoronkova A, Mamoshinaad P, Vanhaelen Q, et al. Artificial intelligence for aging and longevity research: Recent advances and perspectives. *Ageing Res. Rev.* January 2019;49:49–66.

72 Shen MW, Arbab M, Hsu JY, et al. Predictable and precise template-free CRISPR editing of pathogenic variants [published correction appears in. *Nature.* March 2019;567(7746):E1–E2.

73 Klichinsky M, Ruella M, Shestova O, et al. Human chimeric antigen receptor macrophages for cancer immunotherapy. *Nat Biotechnol.* 2020;38:947–953. doi: 10.1038/s41587-020-0462-y.

74 Dzobo K, Adotey S, Thomford NE, et al. Integrating artificial and human intelligence: A partnership for responsible innovation in biomedical engineering and medicine. *OMICS.* May 7, 2020;24(5). doi:10.1089/omi.2019.0038.

75 Poleszczuk J, Enderling H. The optimal radiation dose to induce robust systemic anti-tumor immunity. *Int J Mol Sci.* 2018:19(11):3377. doi: 10.3390/ijms19113377.

5

AI AND IMMUNOLOGY CONSIDERATIONS IN PANDEMICS AND SARS-CoV-2 COVID-19

INTRODUCTION

This chapter is being written in the second half of the year 2020. As we are all painfully aware, the world was struck by a virulent and highly contagious form of a coronavirus, referred to as the "novel coronavirus" at the end of 2019. During the months that followed, this SARS-CoV-2 virus evolved into a global pandemic referred to as COVID-19. It's a sad yet fortuitous coincidence that this book is being written and published during such troubled times. Along with the associated bioscience and public health issues regarding COVID-19, immunology, artificial intelligence (AI) and their relationship are in fact among the most relevant subjects in addressing such a pernicious disease and the physical, emotional, and mental trauma it effectuates. It's regretable that any book related to something as calamitous as an uncontrolled, worldwide, infectious pandemic needs be written at all. The coincidence, however, of such a book written at a time that can enlighten readers to the intimate relationship that AI and the science of immunology bring to this human tragedy can't be overstated. It must be regarded as an opportunity to provide humanity with hope and a greater understanding of how AI and immunology will help eliminate this dreadful disease and restore our personal well-being and the public health.

A reasonable understanding of a ubiquitous and "novel" viral infectious disease, the nature of COVID-19 requires first a brief historical background on contagious infections and pandemics. Then we will address the pathogenesis of viral infections and specifically the immunologic and immunogenic mechanisms and theories of SARS-CoV-2, followed by the clinical diagnostic and therapeutic considerations of coronavirus infections. Finally, we will present and address the profound epidemiologic and public health implications associated with the COVID-19 global pandemic. Through all of these discussions, as in previous chapters, we will include five current reviews and research of AI relevant to each of the topics discussed, albeit a fraction of the body of literature already evolving on the topic. Thus additionally, because of the explosion of AI activity related to the COVID-19 pandemic, we will be referencing numerous AI considerations throughout the narrative text as well.

Much of the discussion in this chapter will have direct relationships to the immunology information from this book's Chapters 2 and 3. The two greatest strengths I feel this chapter brings to the reader as compared to other COVID-19 literature is: (1) it provides an organized summary of all the important and valuable information regarding the immunology of coronavirus and the relevant AI literature on the virus, infectious pandemics, and COVID-19 specifically; and (2) and perhaps its greatest value is that the collective chapters in this book provide immediate access to the most valuable, relevant bioscience information, specifically the science of immunology, on COVID-19 for quick reference. This background information, not included in many books or in most articles addressing COVID-19, provides a fuller understanding of this subject for readers with backgrounds at any level of science, health care or technical (IT) experience.

BACKGROUND CONSIDERATIONS

DEFINITIONS

An endemic level of disease can be defined as that level of observable disease found in a community and considered a baseline or expected level. Occasionally, the expected level of disease may rise, often suddenly, in a defined geographic area and is then termed an "outbreak." If the rise in the cases are grouped in a specific place, it is considered a "cluster," but if they are broadly distributed, it is considered an "epidemic." Finally, pandemic refers to an epidemic that has spread over several countries or continents, usually affecting a large number of people.[1]

Epidemics and pandemics occur when an infectious agent (e.g., a virus) is sufficiently virulent and contagious enough to be conveyed to a large number of susceptible hosts (e.g., humans). These conditions may result from:

- A recent increase in amount or virulence of the agent;
- The recent introduction of the agent into a setting where it has not been before;
- An enhanced mode of transmission so that more susceptible persons are exposed;
- A change in the susceptibility of the host response to the agent; and/or
- Factors that increase host exposure or involve introduction through new portals of entry.[2]

HISTORY OF PANDEMICS

HISTORICAL OVERVIEW

Outbreaks of infectious disease have shaped the economic, political, and social aspects of human civilization, their effects often lasting for centuries. These outbreaks have defined some of the basic tenets of modern medicine with the development of the principles of epidemiology, prevention, immunization, and the field of public health. Throughout history, pandemic outbreaks have decimated societies, determined outcomes of wars, wiped out entire populations, yet paradoxically, they have ushered in new innovations, created and advanced sciences including medicine, immunology, genetics, public health as well as fields of economics and political science systems.[3]

The best-known examples of recorded plagues are those referred to in religious writings starting with the Old Testament. The Athenian plague is an historically documented event that occurred in 430–26 B.C. during the Peloponnesian War. This plague affected a majority of the inhabitants of the overcrowded city-state and claimed lives of more than 25% of the population.[4] Subsequent plagues over the centuries effected the Roman Empire (the Antonine plague),[5] the Justinian plague[6] and forward to 13th century and the Black Plague, a global outbreak of the bubonic plague that originated in China in 1334, arrived in Europe in 1347, and over the following 50 years it reduced the global population from 450 million to possibly below 300 million. Some estimates claim that the Black Death claimed up to 60% of lives in Europe at that time.[7]

RECENT HISTORY

Three influenza pandemics occurred at intervals of several decades during the 20th century, the most severe of which was the so-called "Spanish Flu" (caused by an A[H1N1] virus), estimated to have caused 20–50 million deaths in 1918–1919. Milder pandemics occurred subsequently in 1957–1958 (the "Asian Flu" caused by an A[H2N2] virus) and in 1968 (the "Hong Kong Flu" caused by an A[H3N2] virus), which were estimated to have caused one to four million deaths each.

Polio (classified as an epidemic) occurred in the United States from 1916 to its peak in 1952. Of the 57,628 reported cases, there were 3,145 deaths. Dr. Jonas Salk developed a vaccine and in 1962, the average number of cases dropped to 910. The CDC Trusted Source reports that the United States has been polio-free since 1979.[8] Unfortunately, there have been recent reports of new cases of polio developing in industrialized and developing countries.[9]

First documented case of the human immunosuppressive virus (HIV) occurred in 1981. The pandemic first appeared to be a rare lung infection originating in Africa. Now it is known that it damages the body's immune system and compromises its ability to fight off infections. Acquired immune deficiency syndrome (AIDS) is the final stage of HIV and the 6th leading cause of death in the United States among people 25–44 years old. While no cure currently exists, treatment drugs have been developed and the number of deaths has fallen to 19% since 2005.[10]

The first influenza pandemic of the 21st century occurred in 2009–2010 and was caused by an influenza A(H1N1) virus. This H1N1 pandemic was a reprise of the "Spanish flu" pandemic from 1918, but with far less devastating consequences, thanks to improved epidemiology and public health measures,. Suspected as a re-assortment of bird, swine, and human flu viruses, it was coined the "swine flu."[11] For the first time, a pandemic vaccine was developed, produced, and deployed in multiple countries during the first year of the pandemic. While most cases of pandemic H1N1 were mild, globally it is estimated that this 2009 pandemic caused between 100,000 and 400,000 deaths in the first year alone.[12] Other prominent epidemics and pandemics that occurred in the early 21st century included Ebola, Lassa fever, Middle East respiratory syndrome coronavirus (MERS-CoV), Nipah and henipa virus diseases, Zika, and others.[13]

The first outbreak of Severe Acute Respiratory Syndrome (SARS) was at the start of the 21st century. It was caused by the SARS Corona virus (SARS-CoV-1) and started in China. It affected fewer than 10,000 individuals, mainly in China and Hong Kong, but also in other countries, including 251 cases in Canada (Toronto). The severity of respiratory symptoms and mortality rate of about 10% caused a global public health concern. Through the vigilance of public health systems worldwide, the outbreak was contained by mid-2003.[14] This certainly is a sad statement when considering the virtually uncontrolled evolution and spread of the SARS-CoV-2 pandemic being experienced during the second and into the third decade of the 21st century. How can this have happened ("rhetorical question")? The novel coronavirus (SARS-CoV-2), albeit more contagious than the SARS-CoV-1, was allowed to spread uncontrolled because of inadequate (personal responsibility and political accountability) attention to the simplest cardinal public health measures to control infectious disease – testing, quarantine, social distancing, copious hygiene (hand-washing), wearing masks, and contact tracing. Such a sad statement has resulted in otherwise avoidable death and human suffering.[15]

INCIDENCE AND PREVALENCE OF COVID-19

Originating in the City of Wuhan, China, in December 2019, the novel coronavirus spread rapidly throughout China (epidemic), and within two months, it had spread throughout the entire world becoming a pandemic labeled COVID-19. At the time of this copyediting (November, 2020) this pandemic had spread to 213 countries and territories and has escalated to a total of 60,500,476 reported cases and 1,422,647 deaths worldwide and in the United States, 13,025,277 cases or 21.5% of the worldwide total and 266,844 deaths or 18.8% of the world's total.[16,17] In the United States, COVID-19 has already become the 3rd leading cause of death in 2020, behind heart disease and cancer. There is little doubt that when you read this book, these case numbers and mortality rates will have grown substantially, hopefully less than currently predicted.

PATHOGENESIS, IMMUNOLOGIC AND IMMUNOGENIC CONSIDERATIONS FOR SARS-CoV-2

MECHANISMS

Viruses are not living cells or organisms. They are obligate parasites that lack metabolic machinery of their own to generate energy or to synthesize proteins. Rather, they require a living host (an "obligate") to exploit or infect (enter) so they can replicate to complete their life cycle (see Figure 5.1 and Life Cycle below). The invading virus uses either its genomic DNA or RNA to replicate in the host cell. Coronaviruses (CoV) are a family of RNA viruses that typically cause mild respiratory disease in humans. They include MERS-CoV and SARS-CoV-1, thought to be driven by the spillover of bat-adapted CoVs into an intermediate host (see below). The novel coronavirus (SARS-CoV-2) is a single positive-strand RNA virus. Thus, these viruses are poorly adapted to the human host and if transmitted to humans (e.g., SARS-CoV-2), they are generally associated with more severe clinical presentations. Also, if infection occurs, it can be highly transmissible from person to person as SARS-CoV-2 has demonstrated.[18]

THEORIES

Several studies suggest that antibodies against non-SARS-CoVs are highly prevalent in the general population including children, suggesting that most individuals have been infected by CoVs and have potentially developed a certain degree of (protective) immunity.[19] The severity and the clinical events in some SARS-CoV-2 infections could be related to the activation of an exaggerated, combined immune reaction ("cytokine storm"), causing uncontrolled inflammation (i.e., the immune system as "our worst enemy"). The hypothesis that SARS-CoV-1 (or other, antigenically similar CoV-1) have silently infected a significant proportion of the population, inducing a form of herd immunity (see "Treatment and management strategies" below) has not been confirmed nor apparent in the current pandemic.

Immunity against the infection or patterns of semi-immunity (capacity of the immune system to avoid severe infection) may be due to cellular rather than humoral immune responses.

Within 19 days after symptom onset, a total of 100% of 285 patients with COVID-19 tested positive for antiviral immunoglobulin-G (IgG). Seroconversion for IgG and IgM (transition of the test results for IgG or IgM against SARS-CoV-2 from negative to positive results in sequential samples) occurred simultaneously or sequentially. Both IgG and IgM titers plateaued within six days after seroconversion.[20] Thus, serological testing may be helpful for the diagnosis of suspected patients with negative RT-PCR results and for the identification of asymptomatic infections.

Animal models suggest that the efficiency of T lymphocyte-mediated immune responses (see Section "Innate (Natural) Immunity", in Chapter 2, page 16) is pivotal for controlling SARS-CoV infections.[21] There are currently no data on the specific role of either humoral or cellular immunity or innate immunity in patients recovering from COVID-19. T lymphocytes responsible for clinically relevant antiviral immune responses have a significant chance to be locally present in, or close to, respiratory epithelia.[22] As such, it is very possible that the exclusive detection of humoral immunity against SARS-CoV-2 leads to an underestimation of the anti-SARS-CoV-2 cellular immune responses. It becomes plausible that, after infection by SARS-CoV-2, a sort of race decides the course of the events. Either a cellular innate immune response rapidly clears SARS-CoV-2 without any (or mild) clinical signs of infection, or the virus causes a state of immunosuppression that debilitates and sometimes overwhelms the host's defense.[23]

Researchers have analyzed genomic data related to the overall molecular structure of the new coronavirus. Their testing (AI machine learning karyotyping analysis) has traced this novel coronavirus to a strain of Malaysian anteater (pangolin) containing genomic regions that are very closely related to the human virus. Their analysis showed that the genome resembles that of a bat coronavirus discovered after the COVID-19 pandemic began. However, in "SARS-CoV-2 testing," the binding region of the spike protein also resembles the novel virus found in pangolins (anteaters). This provides additional evidence that the coronavirus that causes COVID-19 almost certainly originated in nature, most likely in bats with an intermediate animal (anteater or monkey?) host and ultimately transmitted to humans ("zoonotic spillover").[25]

Most important among these findings is the receptor binding domain (spike protein) that dictates how the virus is able to attach and infect human cells (see Life Cycle below). This comparative analysis of genomic data dispelled the postulate that the virus was laboratory constructed or was a "manipulated" virus. Rather, it promotes a lesson learned to reduce human exposure to wildlife and to ban the trade and consumption (e.g., "wet markets" in China) of wildlife. This genetic information concludes that "coronaviruses clearly have the capacity to jump species boundaries and adapt to new hosts (virus recently reported in Malaysian tigers in Bronx Zoo),[26] making it straightforward to predict that more will emerge in the future." However, as not all of the early COVID-19 cases were wet market associated, it is possible that the emerging story is more complicated than first suspected.

The genomic data of the new coronavirus responsible for COVID-19 show that its spike protein contains some unique adaptations. One of these adaptations provides special ability of this coronavirus to bind to a specific protein on human cells called angiotensin converting enzyme (ACE-2). Human ACE-2 is expressed in epithelial cells of the lung and serve as an entry receptor site for SARS-CoV-2 spike glycoprotein.[27] ACE-2 genetic polymorphism (occurrence of different forms in the life cycle of an individual organism) represented by diverse genetic variants in the human genome has been shown to affect virus-binding activity[28] suggesting a possible genetic predisposition to COVID-19 infection. Thus, machine learning analysis of genetic variants from asymptomatic, mild, or severe COVID-19 patients can be performed to classify and predict people based on their vulnerability or resistance to potential COVID-19 infection. Furthermore, the machine learning model can also return those prioritized genetic variants, such as ACE-2 polymorphism.

The entire genome of the 2019-novel coronavirus is more than 80% similar to the previous human SARS-like bat CoV. Thus, previously used animal models for SARS-CoV can be utilized to study the infectious pathogenicity of SARS-CoV-2. CRISPR-mediated (see Section "CRISPR-Cas9 (Gene Editing)", Chapter 4, page 77 and below), genetically modified hamsters or other small animals can be utilized for the study of the pathogenicity of novel coronaviruses. In such studies, AI predictions can be used to investigate the inhibitory role of the drug against SARS-CoV-2.[29]

LIFE CYCLE OF SARS-CoV-2

The life cycle of SARS-CoV-2 captures the essence of molecular biology, immunogenetics and immunogenomics in its extracellular and intracellular stages of infection and proliferation. At the extracellular level the virus demonstrates classic and "novel" characteristics. First, the classic extracellular immunologic infectious process of receptors on an antigen surface (in this case, the virus) binding to receptors on a cell wall. The novel aspect here is the unique SARS-CoV-2 spike protein receptors binding to ACE-2 cell wall receptors allowing the virus to penetrate the cell wall.

At the intracellular level, the viral genomic RNA releases its genetic material into the cell's cytoplasm producing the classic steps of transcription into multiple proteins (proteolysis) that replicate and translate into the genomic RNA of a new viral particle including a "novel" spike protein envelope. From here, the+strand genomic RNA combines with the mechanics of the endoplasmic reticulum of the cytoplasm (golgi apparatus, ribosomes, etc.) to produce a new viral particle which exits the cell (exocytosis) and moves on to infect more host cells.

Figure 5.1 identifies and traces each step in this life-cycle process:

1 When the spike protein of SARS-CoV-2 binds to the ACE-2 receptor of the host cell, the virus enters the cell;
2 Then the fatty envelope of the virus is peeled off, which releases the viral genomic RNA into the cytoplasm;
3 The ORF1a and ORF1b (genes) RNAs are produced by genomic RNA, and then translated into pp1a and pp1ab proteins, respectively;

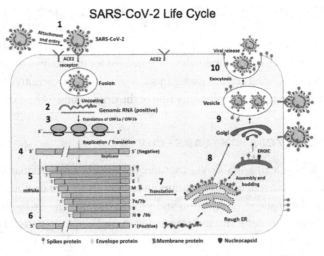

Figure 5.1 SARS-CoV-2 life cycle. (Shereen MA, Khana S, Kazmi A, et al. COVID-19 infection: Origin, transmission, and characteristics of human coronaviruses. *J. Adv. Res.* July 2020;24:91–98.)

4 Protein pp1a and ppa1b are cleaved by protease (proteolysis) to make a total of 16 nonstructural proteins;

5 Some of the nonstructural proteins form a replication/transcription complex (RNA-dependent RNA polymerase, RdRp), which use the (+) strand genomic RNA as a template;

6 The (+) strand genomic RNA produced through the replication process becomes the genome of a new virus particle;

7 Subgenomic RNAs produced through the transcription are translated into structural proteins (S: spike protein, E: envelope protein, M: membrane protein, and N: nucleocapsid protein) which form a viral particle;

8 Spike, envelope, and membrane proteins enter the endoplasmic reticulum, and the nucleocapsid protein is combined with the (+) strand genomic RNA to become a nucleoprotein complex;

9 This complex merges into the complete virus particle in the endoplasmic reticulum-Golgi apparatus compartment; and

10 The new viral particles are released (exocytosis) to extracellular region through the Golgi apparatus and the vesicle.

REVIEW OF AI REGARDING THE PATHOGENESIS OF SARS-CoV-2

1 *Forbes Magazine* reported on a global artificial intelligence database company, BlueDot, using an AI-powered algorithm, machine learning, and natural-language processing to analyze information from a multitude of sources that can track over a 100 infectious diseases.[30]

2 AI is playing an important role in evaluating the pathogenesis, diagnosis, and treatment of the SARS-CoV-2 virus. There is an urgent need to develop a system with AI-based machine learning capacity to analyze and integrate imaging-based, patient-based, clinician-based, and molecular measurements-based data, to fight the outbreak of COVID-19 and enable more efficient responses to unknown infections in the future.[31]

3 Vaxign (see also Vaccines, page 110) is a reverse vaccinology tool being used with Vaxign-ML machine learning tool to predict

COVID-19 vaccine candidates. A study applied the state-of-the-art Vaxign reserve vaccinology (RV) and Vaxign-ML machine learning strategies to the entire SARS-CoV-2 proteomes including both structural and non-structural proteins for vaccine candidate prediction. The results indicate for the first time that many non-structural proteins could be used as potential vaccine candidates.[32]

4 AI technologies are powerful tools against COVID-19 and widely used in combating this pandemic. A survey investigated the main scope and contributions of AI in combating COVID-19 from the aspects of disease detection and diagnosis, virology and pathogenesis, drug and vaccine development, and epidemic and transmission prediction. AI mainly focuses on medical image inspection, genomics, drug development, and transmission prediction, and thus still has great potential in this field.[33]

5 On March 16, 2020, the White House issued a call to action for global AI researchers to develop new algorithms and data mining techniques to assist in COVID-19-related research. Within a short period of time advanced machine learning techniques were developed and implemented to better understand the pattern of viral spread, further improve diagnostic speed and accuracy, develop novel effective therapeutic approaches, and potentially identify the most susceptible people based on personalized genetic and physiological characteristics. This is only the beginning of a permanent role AI will play in global health care.[34]

CLINICAL CONSIDERATIONS FOR CORONAVIRUS (SARS-CoV-2) INFECTION

CLINICAL MANIFESTATIONS (SIGNS AND SYMPTOMS)

Reported illnesses with the novel coronavirus have ranged from mild symptoms to severe illness and death for confirmed COVID-19 cases. The symptoms may appear 2–14 days after exposure (based on the incubation period of SARS-CoV viruses). Symptoms include fever, cough, and shortness of breath. Elderly and immune compromised patients are at greater risk for contracting the virus and for poor outcomes. However, significant numbers of young and healthy people are also being reported, though generally with better outcomes. Spread occurs through respiratory droplets produced when an infected person coughs or sneezes. These droplets can land in the mouths or noses of people who are nearby or possibly be inhaled into the lungs.

Older age, obesity, and comorbidities have consistently been reported as risk factors for unfavorable prognosis and prolonged symptomatology ("long-haulers syndrome"). Less clear so far has been how the number and types of comorbidities influence the outcome. An epidemiologic clarification was provided through a nationwide Chinese retrospective cohort study involving 1590 PCR-confirmed (see Antigen testing below) COVID-19 cases (mean age, 49 years; 43% female) diagnosed between December 11, 2019, and January 31, 2020. The most common symptoms were fever, dry cough, and fatigue (88%, 70%, and 43%, respectively). The mean incubation period was four days. According to the 2007 American Thoracic Society/Infectious Disease Society of America guideline for community-acquired pneumonia criteria, 16% of the cases were considered severe. Reported proportions with comorbidities included 17% hypertension, 8% diabetes, 4% cardiovascular disease, 2% cerebrovascular disease, 2% chronic obstructive pulmonary disease (COPD), 1% chronic kidney disease, and 1% malignancy. At least one comorbidity was significantly more common in severe than in non-severe cases (33% vs. 10%).[35] Obesity puts those with coronavirus disease 2019 (COVID-19) at particularly high risk of death, more so than related risk factors such as diabetes or hypertension, according to a study of patient records by researchers from Kaiser Permanente.[36]

As described above (page 94), coronavirus disease leads to fast activation of innate immune cells, especially in patients developing severe disease. Innate immune activation, levels of many pro-inflammatory effector cytokines (e.g., TNF, IL-1β, IL-6, IL-8, G-CSF, and GM-CSF), as well as higher levels of chemokines (e.g., MCP1, IP10, and MIP1α) are also found in those who are critically ill. In addition, the levels of some T-cell-derived cytokines (e.g., IL-17) are increased.[37] A cytokine storm (see Chapter 2, page 22) develops that triggers a hyperinflammatory state. As stated above and in Chapters 3 and 4, this chronic inflammatory clinical response leaves virtually all organ systems vulnerable to adverse effects from the novel coronavirus. Of increasing concern are the cardiovascular effects resulting from perivasculitis (inflammation of the adventitia and endothelial lining of blood vessel walls – see Chapter 4, page 60).[38] Anti-inflammatories (steroids) and cytokine inhibitor drugs (e.g., checkpoint inhibitors, IgG, Interleukin 6 blockers – from right side of the "Inflammatory Cascade," Chapter 2, Figure 2.3 and Chapter 3, Table 3.2) are being studied and beginning to show some benefits in advanced cases and late stage disease.[39]

AI is playing an important role in evaluating the pathogenesis, diagnosis, and treatment of the SARS-CoV-2 virus. There is an urgent need to develop a system with AI-based machine learning capacity to analyze and integrate imaging-based, patient-based, clinician-based, and molecular measurements-based data, to fight the outbreak of COVID-19 and enable more efficient responses to unknown infections in the future.[40]

DIAGNOSTIC TESTING

The clarion call during the early stages of the COVID-19 pandemic was "Testing, Testing, Testing." Tracking ("contact tracing") an invisible virus is the only way to control it, and the most effective strategy to accomplish that goal starts with building a comprehensive system to test anyone who may be infected. Upon accomplishing that, then those positive cases can be isolated and "contact traced" (identifying persons who may have come into contact with the infected person) and testing them as well and isolate all positive cases. This critical "diagnostic" process is conducted through three types of tests, two testing for the antigen (people who are currently infected) and a third, testing for antibodies to the antigen (people previously infected who have developed antibodies to the virus).

Continuing efforts are being made to develop novel diagnostic approaches to COVID-19 using machine learning algorithms. Machine learning-based screening of SARS-CoV-2 assay designs using a CRISPR-based virus detection system (see Section "CRISPR-Cas9 (Gene Editing)" Chapter 4, page 77) are demonstrating high sensitivity and speed. Neural network classifiers have been developed for a large-scale screening of COVID-19 patients based on their distinct respiratory pattern. Also, a deep-learning-based analysis system of thoracic CT images was constructed for automated detection and monitoring of COVID-19 patients over time. Rapid development of automated diagnostic systems based on AI and machine learning can not only contribute to increased diagnostic accuracy and speed, but will also protect health care workers by decreasing their contacts with COVID-19 patients.

ANTIGEN TESTING

An antigen test reveals if a person is actively infected with the SARS-CoV-2 virus. The test detects certain proteins that are part of the virus. Using a nasal or throat swab to get a fluid sample, antigen tests can produce results in minutes. Because these tests are faster and less expensive than molecular tests (below), some experts consider antigen tests more practical to use for large numbers of people. Once the infection has gone, the antigen disappears. A positive antigen test result is considered very accurate, but there's an increased chance of false negative results, meaning it's possible to be infected with the virus but have negative antigen test results. So antigen tests aren't as sensitive as molecular tests. Antigen tests already exist for strep throat, influenza, tuberculosis, HIV, and other infectious diseases and thus, are readily available.[41]

MOLECULAR GENETIC TEST (PCR TEST)

This antigen test is considered the gold standard in that it detects genetic material of the virus using a lab technique called polymerase chain reaction (PCR). Also called a PCR test, a health care worker collects fluid from a nasal or throat swab or from saliva. Results may be available in minutes if analyzed onsite or one to two days if sent to an outside lab. Molecular tests are considered very accurate when properly performed by a health care professional, but the rapid form of the test appears to miss some cases. The FDA also approved certain COVID-19 at-home test kits, available only with doctor approval. It can be done with a nasal swab kit or a saliva kit. The sample is mailed to a lab for testing. The FDA warns consumers against buying unapproved home tests because they may be inaccurate and unsafe.[42]

ANTIBODY TESTING

Antibody tests check a person's blood by looking for antibodies, which may (or may not) tell if the person had a past infection with the coronavirus. Antibodies are proteins that help fight off infections and thus, can provide immunity and protection against getting the infection again (see Chapter 2). Neutralizing antibodies are specific to an antigen (the virus) and thus, provide protection only against the specific disease associated with the antigen (in the case of coronavirus as the antigen, the disease being COVID-19). If the person is exposed to the antigen (coronavirus) again, the antibodies produce "memory" (anamnestic protection) toward the disease.[43] However, there are increasing reports of reinfection with the novel coronavirus suggesting that some coronavirus antibodies may not be neutralizing nor persist for extended periods.[44]

Except in instances in which viral testing is delayed, antibody tests should not be used to diagnose a current COVID-19 infection. An antibody test may not show if you have a current COVID-19 infection because it can take one to three weeks after infection for your body to make antibodies. To see if you are currently infected, you need a viral test. Viral (antigen) tests described above identify the virus in samples from your respiratory system, such as a swab from the inside of your nose. It is possible to isolate the coronavirus from respiratory secretions, blood, urine, and fecal samples for diagnostic testing. Clinically, infections can be diagnosed with respiratory viral panels that are widely commercially available.[45]

TREATMENT AND MANAGEMENT STRATEGIES

Care for coronavirus patients is supportive in nature and may include supplemental oxygen, fluid administration, and, for critically ill patients, being managed in intensive care units and receiving rescue therapies such as extracorporeal membrane oxygenation (pulmonary ventilation). Stringent infection control is critical to preventing transmission to health care workers and other patients. Droplet precautions (e.g., personal protective equipment [PPE] including surgical or procedure mask, gown, and gloves) are indicated during the treatment of all coronavirus patients, and such protocols for droplet-spread respiratory viruses are part of hospital infection control practices. Additional respiratory precautions may also be appropriate during aerosol-generating procedures (such include loud talking, singing, and of course coughing and sneezing).[46]

At the time of the writing of this chapter on COVID-19, treatment and management strategies continue to grow, some proving effective and some ineffective. In that this is being written at the height of the pandemic (late 2020), it must be considered a prospective view of appropriate treatment and management as recommended by the medical experts guiding us through this difficult period. It will be of interest to the readers in the months and years ahead, to evaluate retrospectively, which of these treatment and management approaches proved most valuable. Hopefully, it will be a prescient lesson to future generations in their preparedness and response to epidemics and pandemics they may face. Future readers of this book will be able to retrospectively assess the strengths and weaknesses of each.

GENERAL MEASURES

Basic Preventive Steps

1 Shelter-in-place or "self-isolation" (remain in your home with only absolutely necessary outdoor activities);
2 Social distancing (separation of > six feet between people);
3 Avoid large gatherings (greater than 5 to 10 people);
4 Wash your hands copiously and frequently;
5 Face masks (first CDC and surgeon general suggest for use only if infected, but subsequently recommended for fulltime use);
6 If symptoms occur (fever, cough, chills, aches, and pains), get tested and if positive, self-quarantine for minimum 14 days and retest x2 before assuming normal activities;
7 If symptoms advance over two to three days, seek medical attention.

Mitigation

All of the procedures and policies to reduce risks of infectious spread are categorized as "mitigation." Results of mitigation are measured by "flattening the (modeling) curve" (the inverted bellshaped curve measuring daily cases and mortality).

Contact Tracing

Epidemiologists, or "disease detectives," start with the index patient, sometimes called "patient zero." Depending on what they already know about that patient's condition – how the disease is spread, its natural history, what symptoms it causes – they interview the patient to learn about their movements and identify all close contacts (persons, places, and things). Based on the answers, public health workers contact each associated person to explain their risk, offer screening for the infection and conduct regular monitoring for symptoms of the infection. This important public health measure is not progressing well (late 2020) due to limited "tracer personnel" and public resistance to sharing information.

Modeling

1   Study the mechanisms by which disease is spreading;
2   Monitor (graphically) through testing positive case volumes, death rates, and other vital statiistics;[47]
3   Graphically modeling cases also provides rates of positive cases which is a strong indicator of control of spread;
4   Predict the future course of an outbreak; and
5   Evaluate strategies to control an epidemic. Modeling data produces an inverted bell-shaped curve with the x-axis representing time and the y-axis representing number of cases.

Herd Immunity and R Naught (RO or R_o)

The concept of herd immunity is an epidemiological formula in which a sufficient amount of people are immunized or vaccinated against a pathogen, thus reducing the rate of infection throughout the population. The vaccination levels must produce a threshold called the "R-Naught" or R_O (The SIR ['susceptible-infectious-recovered']) formulation, a factor that determines the transmissibility of the pathogen. It denotes the average number of secondary cases of an infectious disease that one case would generate in a completely susceptible population. That is, when one infected person infects greater than one other person, a potential exponential increase in infections results leading to an epidemic or pandemic. If, however, transmission on average remains below an R_O of one person, this will result in a decreasing spread in infection and eventually into a majority of the population (an estimated 60%–70% needed) to produce "herd immunity."[48]

In the absence of a vaccine, developing herd immunity to an infectious agent requires large amounts of people actually being infected, developing antibodies to the infectious agent and thus, becoming immunized against future infection. Scientists are not always certain if this immunity is permanent or for how long it might last. But even assuming that immunity is long-lasting, a very large number of people must be infected to reach the 60%–70% herd immunity threshold required. During this process, mortality of certain infections like SARS-CoV-2 could reach unacceptable levels as has occurred in Sweden.[49]

Nor does a pathogen magically disappear when the herd immunity threshold is reached. Rather, it only means that transmission begins to slow down and that a new epidemic is unlikely to start up again. An uncontrolled pandemic could continue for months after herd immunity is reached, potentially infecting many more millions in the process. These additional infections are what epidemiologists refer to as "overshoot."[50]

THERAPEUTICS

The goal of therapeutic interventions in infectious disease is to eliminate the antigen (in the case of COVID-19, eliminating the coronavirus) and restoring the patient back to health and their immune system back to a REGULATED, innate versus a dysregulated (see Chapters 2 and 3), adaptive level. These therapeutic interventions are achieved through extracellular attacks on the virus through chemotherapeutic and molecular biologic approaches, intracellular molecular biologic interventions, and combined approaches. The following are the general categories of each of these therapeutic strategies.

Monoclonal Antibodies

Monoclonal antibodies (any drug with the name suffix, "…mab") are laboratory engineered antibodies used to mimic the immune system's own antibodies for a specific antigen (see Chapter 3, page 44). These antibodies are made by identical immune cells that are all clones of a unique parent cell. Monoclonal antibodies can have monovalent affinity, in that they bind to the same epitope (the part of an antigen that is recognized by the antibody). Rather than wait for vaccines to coax the body to make its own antibodies, scientists are studying versions of these molecules to directly disable the SARS-CoV-2 coronavirus at the extracellular level.[51]

Monoclonal antibodies are nowadays often generated by isolating or transforming antibody-producing cells taken directly from immunized animals or patients, and transplanting the antibody-encoding genes of these cells into suitable producer cell lines, rather than using hybridoma technology.[52] San Francisco-based Vir Biotechnology has identified several human neutralizing monoclonal antibody (mAb) candidates against SARS-CoV-2. The lead antibody's ability to neutralize the SARS-CoV-2 live virus has been confirmed in two different laboratories. It binds to an epitope, the specific site on the viral antigen molecule that is also seen on the SARS-CoV-1 virus that causes SARS. This means the antigen is highly conserved and less likely to disappear should the viruses mutate or develop resistance to the antibody.[24]

Current results (late 2020) with monoclonal antibody therapies has produced mixed results with benefits mostly realized in late stage and severe infections. One monoclonal antibody, Regeneron's REGN-CoV2 has already (November, 2020) received FDA "Emergency Use Authorization."

Convalescent Plasma (Serum)

Another extracellular antibody strategy uses plasma collected from patients who recovered from COVID-19. Each donates a pint of blood. The red and white blood cells are separated and put back into the donor's bloodstream while the blood plasma, rich with virus-fighting antibodies, is kept aside.[53] Four hundred and three monoclonal antibodies were isolated from three convalescent COVID-19 patients. They showed that the patients had strong immune responses against the viral spike protein, the complex that binds to receptors on the host cell. A subset of antibodies was able to neutralize the virus.[54] Early results (late 2020) are proving questionable.

Hydroxychloroquine (Plaquenil®) combined with Azithromycin (Zithromax®)

A small sample survey showed that hydroxychloroquine (a biologic) treatment is associated with viral load reduction in COVID-19 patients and its effect is reinforced by azithromycin (an antibiotic). Unfortunately, this therapeutic approach gained support and was heavily politicized in the United States during the early stages of the pandemic with only anecdotal evidence and no scientific or clinical validating evidence. Subsequently, a study reported in the New England Journal of Medicine (and others afterwards) concluded that results do not support the use of hydroxychloroquine at present, outside randomized clinical trials testing its efficacy.[55] Further work may (or may not) be warranted to determine if these compounds could be useful as chemoprophylaxis to prevent the transmission of the virus without significant adverse effects.[56]

Remdesivir

This drug is thought to interfere with the intracellular mechanism that coronavirus uses to make copies of itself (see Figure 5.1 and discussion on Life Cycle above). Scientists are still working out exactly how that occurs. A preliminary report published in *The New England Journal of Medicine* showed that the drug shortened recovery time for people with COVID-19 from an average of 15 days to about 11 days.[57] This drug (Gilead's Veklury®) is one of the earliest drugs to receive FDA approval in late 2020.

Dexamethasone (and Corticosteroids)

As discussed above and in detail in Chapter 4, chronic inflammatory organ injury (e.g., heart, lungs, kidneys) may occur in severe COVID-19, with a subgroup of patients having markedly elevated levels of inflammatory markers. Several therapeutic interventions have been proposed to mitigate inflammatory organ injury in viral pneumonia including glucocorticoids (i.e., dexamethasone). Glucocorticoids have been widely used in syndromes closely related to COVID-19, including SARS, Middle East respiratory syndrome (MERS), severe influenza, and community-acquired pneumonia. However, the evidence to support or discourage the use of glucocorticoids under these conditions has been weak.[58] In patients hospitalized with COVID-19, the use of dexamethasone resulted in lower 28-day mortality among those who were receiving either invasive mechanical ventilation or oxygen alone at randomization but not among those receiving no respiratory support.[59] Other steroids are also beginning to show some promising results.[60]

VACCINES (IMMUNIZATION)

By definition, the traditional vaccine is a biological preparation that provides active, adaptive immunity to a particular infectious disease (e.g., SARS-CoV-2) by stimulating antibodies to the source of the infection. It typically contains an agent that resembles the disease-causing microorganism made from weakened or killed forms of the microbe (an attenuated virus), its toxins, or one of its surface proteins. The spike protein is the target for most of the COVID-19 vaccine human clinical trials and so research centers on how the immune system, particularly B- and T-cells, responds to the spike protein. B-cells are responsible for producing the antibodies that recognize SARS-CoV-2, while T-cells play an important role in supporting the development of the B-cell response (see Chapter 2).

A vaccine is a biological preparation that provides active, adaptive immunity to a particular infectious disease (e.g., SARS-CoV-2). Vaccination is the act of getting a vaccine, usually as an injection to immunize a person (immunization) to protect against a disease. Testing for an effective vaccine begins with giving the vaccine to animals such as mice or monkeys to see if it produces an immune response. Then Phase One vaccinates a small number of people to test safety and dosage as well as to confirm that it stimulates the immune system. Phase Two includes hundreds of people split into groups (viral injected and placebo), such as children and the elderly, to see if the vaccine acts differently in them as well as safety and ability to stimulate the immune system. Phase Three gives the vaccine to thousands of people (again, two groups) to see how many become infected, compared with volunteers who received a placebo. These trials can determine any rare side effects that might be missed in earlier studies. Finally, if the vaccine protects against the coronavirus in at least 50% of vaccinated people it is considered effective and regulators decide whether to approve the vaccine or not. During a pandemic, a vaccine may receive emergency use authorization before getting formal approval.[62]

As the saying goes, "It's not the vaccine, it's the vaccination." Indeed, the production, distribution and delivery from the bottle to the arm is almost as complex as developing the vaccine itself. Given the worldwide nature of COVID-19, the challenge of the logistics necessary for effective and efficient completion of the vaccination process (e.g., some vaccines require deep freezing storage, up to -94°F and multiple dosages [boosters] at 3 week intervals), no less prioritizing the myriad of variables within populations, is a daunting and formidable task, especially when politics gets involved. Nonetheless, the apotheosis of pandemic control and cure lies in the successful and timely execution of a vaccination strategy. Vaxign (see AI Review, page 97) is a tool using machine learning to predict COVID-19 vaccine candidates. This is one of many tools the public health sector and AI must and will analyze (big data analytics), develop and implement the most effective channels of vaccine distribution.

In response to the COVID-19 pandemic, vaccinology has expanded rapidly from traditional approaches to new molecular biological technologies that are showing strong potential. The following categories of vaccines include the traditional and the newest (as of late 2020) technologies.

Anti-Idiotype Regulatory Loop

Way back in Chapter 2 (page 21) and (page 46) we discussed the very complex system of idiotype antigen-specific B cells increasing through genetic cloning and creating their own immunogenic stimuli which induces anti-idiotype-specific antibodies ("antibodies 1, 2"). This produces an antibody idiotype-specific regulatory circuit also referred to as the "idiotype network theory" (INT). I mentioned that this "regulatory circuit" remains the center of much immunology research including its potential of it providing long-lasting immunity as a vaccine which it has demonstrated for cancer[89]. To date, there has been little reported on research into this technology's use with SARS-CoV-2, but it is likely that such research is in its early stages and among the 190 plus worldwide investigations into COVID-19 vaccines.

Viral-Vector Recombinant Serotypes

As of late 2020, at least seven teams are developing vaccines using the novel coronavirus itself, in a weakened or inactivated form. Around 25 groups say they are working on viral-vector vaccines. In this technology, a virus such as measles or adenovirus (recombinant serotype Ad5)[63] is genetically engineered so that it can produce coronavirus proteins in the body. One such technology, AstraZeneca's AZD12222 adenovirus, has shown sufficient success to have received FDA "Emergency Use Authorization" in late November, 2020. At least 20 teams are aiming to use genetic instructions (in the form of DNA or RNA) for a coronavirus protein that prompts an immune response. Finally, many researchers are experimenting with injecting coronavirus proteins directly into the body to mimic the coronavirus's outer coat.[64]

Messenger RNA (mRNA)

SARS-CoV-2 is an RNA virus which means its genetic material is encoded in RNA. Once the virus is inside our cells, it releases its

RNA and making long viral proteins to compromise the immune system (see Life Cycle above). An mRNAcontaining a genetic strip (fragment) of the coronavirus genetic material, and genomic transcription and translation produce copies of the spike proteins which initiate an APC/ T_H (T-helper cells) and T_C (T-cytotoxic cells) which ultimately produce B cells that produce antibodies that generate spike protein fragments that abort further proliferation of the virus. Success in vaccine trials with mRNA at the 95% levels as of November, 2020 have led to FDA "Emergency Use Authorization" for Pfizer's BNT162b2 and Moderna's ChAdOx1 mRNA vaccines with anxious anticipation of their distribution by early 2021.

One of the weapons in our cells' is an RNA surveillance mechanism called nonsense-mediated mRNA decay (NMD) that protects us from further genetic mutations that could cause disease. With the progression of new viral strains, mRNA can be easily genetically reprogrammed to recognize mutant viral strains and allows for the development of second generation vaccines that directly target processes critical to a virus's life cycle.[61]

CRISPR-Cas13 and RNA Screening

A new Cas13 RNA screen has been developed to establish guide RNAs for the COVID-19 coronavirus and human RNA segments which could be used in vaccines, therapeutics, and diagnostics. A novel CRISPR-based (see Section "CRISPR-Cas9 (Gene Editing)", Chapter 4, page 77) editing tool enables researchers to target mRNA and knockout genes without altering the genome has been developed. Using the CRISPR-Cas13 enzyme, researchers have created a genetic screen for RNA, currently designed for use on humans, which they say could also be used on RNA containing viruses and bacteria.

The developers have used their parallel-screening technique to create optimal guide RNAs for the SARS-CoV-2 coronavirus which could be used for future detection and therapeutic applications. The platform is optimized to run massively parallel genetic screens at the RNA level in human cells because it is based on the CRISPR-Cas13 enzyme, which targets RNA instead of DNA. The data are collected by targeting thousands of different sites in human RNA transcripts to create a machine learning-based predictive model to expedite identification of the most effective Cas13 guide RNAs.[65]

AI and immunoinformatics (see below) play a central role in vaccines by suggesting components understanding viral protein structures, and helping medical researchers scour tens of thousands of relevant research papers at an unprecedented pace.[66] AI-supported preclinical studies in mice of a candidate vaccine based on this spike protein are already underway at NIH's Vaccine Research Center (VRC). But there will be many more steps after that to test safety and efficacy, and then to scale up to produce millions of doses. National Institute of Allergy and Infectious Diseases (NIAID) is now working with the numerous biotechnology company (AstraZeneca, Pfizer, J&J, Moderna, et al. as described above) to use the latest findings to develop a vaccine candidate using messenger RNA (mRNA), molecules that serve as templates for making proteins. The goal is to direct the body to produce a spike protein in such a way to elicit an immune response and the production of antibodies. Other forms of vaccine candidates are also in preclinical development.[67]

IMMUNOINFORMATICS (COMPUTATIONAL IMMUNOLOGY)

The explosion of new immunological data through increased research in understanding the immune system, particularly in infectious disease pathogenesis and the application of the knowledge from bioinformatics has led to a better understanding of the importance of the immune system through immunoinformatics (computational immunology). Through increased knowledge of the immune system, AI research, and the cost-effective, specific and effective approaches like *in silico* immunoinformatics (scientific experimentation and research conducted or produced by means of computer modeling or computer simulation),[68] the concerns for emerging and potentially re-surging diseases caused by pathogenic organisms, antigenic variability/complex life cycle of pathogens (see Figure 5.1, COVID-19 life cycle, above), and the need of personalized vaccination can be combated on a molecular level.[69]

AI and immunoinformatics are being used to better understand the structure of proteins involved in SARS-Cov-2 infection in search for potential treatments and vaccines. Proteins have a three-dimensional structure, which is determined by their genetically encoded amino acid sequence (next-gen sequencing of genetic code), and this structure influences the role and function of the protein. An AI Google DeepMind system called AlphaFold[70] uses amino acid sequencing and protein structure to make predictions to construct a "potential of mean force" which can be used to characterize the protein's shape. This system has been applied to predict the structures of six proteins related to SARS-CoV-2.[71]

In silico immunoinformatics depends on experimental science (wet laboratory) to produce raw data for analysis. Thus, its predictions are not formal proofs of any concepts. They do not replace the traditional experimental research methods of actually testing hypotheses. The quality of immunoinformatics predictions depends on the quality of data and the sophistication of the algorithms being used. Sequence data from high-throughput analysis often contain errors. If the sequences are wrong, or annotations incorrect, the results from the downstream analysis could be misleading as well.[72] The future of immunological research will be enhanced by the ability to make discoveries in biologics (e.g., vaccines) more effectively and efficiently through combined AI and in silico immunoinformatics with traditional experimental research methods.

ARTIFICIAL INTELLIGENCE AND DIAGNOSIS

There have been multiple citations regarding AI and COVID-19 in this chapter (5). However, it would not be complete without a direct reference to deep learning and the diagnosis and treatment of the coronavirus. An article dated June 12, 2020 "offers a response to combat the virus through Artificial Intelligence (AI)." It identifies AI platforms for use by physicians and researchers to accelerate the process of diagnosis and treatment of the COVID-19 disease. Some include Deep Learning (DL) methods, Generative Adversarial Networks (GANs), Extreme Learning Machine (ELM), and Long/Short Term Memory (LSTM), and integrated bioinformatics approaches with different aspects of information from a continuum of structured and unstructured data sources.

The main advantage of these AI-based platforms is to accelerate the process of diagnosis and treatment of the COVID-19 disease. The most recent related publications and medical reports were investigated to facilitate reaching a reliable Artificial Neural Network-based tool for challenges associated with COVID-19. There are some specific inputs for each platform, including various forms of the data, such as clinical data and medical imaging which can improve the performance of the introduced approaches toward the best responses in practical applications.[88]

REVIEW OF AI FOR CLINICAL CONSIDERATIONS FOR CORONAVIRUS INFECTIONS

1   Continuing efforts are being made to develop novel diagnostic approaches to COVID-19 using machine learning algorithms. Machine learning-based screening of SARS-CoV-2 assay designs using a CRISPR-based virus detection system (see Cas13 above) are demonstrating high sensitivity and speed. Neural network classifiers have been developed for a large-scale screening of COVID-19 patients based on their distinct respiratory pattern. Also, a deep-learning-based analysis system of thoracic CT images was constructed for automated detection and monitoring of COVID-19 patients over time. Rapid development of

automated diagnostic systems based on AI and machine learning can not only contribute to increased diagnostic accuracy and speed, but will also protect health care workers by decreasing their contacts with COVID-19 patients.[73]

2   Five companies were highlighted for developing deep learning models to predict old and new drugs that might successfully treat COVID-19.[74,90]

3   Advanced deep-learning-based algorithms known as the convolutional neural network plays a great effect on extracting highly essential features, mostly in terms of medical images. This technique, with using CT and X-Ray image scans, has been adopted in most of the recently published articles on the coronavirus with remarkable results. Furthermore, according to this paper, this can be noted and said that deep learning technology has potential clinical applications.[75]

4   A new framework has been proposed to detect COVID-19 using built-in smartphone sensors (IoTs). The proposal provides a low-cost solution that ordinary people can use on their smartphones for the virus detection purposes. The designed AI enabled framework reads the smartphone sensors signal measurements to predict the grade of severity of the pneumonia as well as predicting the result of the disease.[76]

5   AI and deep learning algorithms are being developed to enhance the detection and diagnosis of COVID-19. The need to provide access to accurate and low-cost tests for the diagnosis of COVID-19 is critical. Such AI algorithms can be used as an initial screening tool for suspected cases so that patients at higher risk could have confirmatory laboratory-based tests and be isolated if necessary. These algorithms could help health care providers triage patients with COVID-19 into potentially three groups: the 80% who have mild disease; the 15% who have moderate disease; and the 5% who have severe disease, including those at high risk of mortality. Finally, AI can facilitate the discovery of novel drugs with which to treat COVID-19.[77]

EPIDEMIOLOGY AND PUBLIC HEALTH CONSIDERATIONS IN COVID-19

CURRENT EPIDEMIOLOGIC CONSIDERATIONS

On December 31, 2019, Chinese authorities alerted the World Health Organization of an outbreak of a novel strain of coronavirus causing severe illness, which was named SARS-CoV-2 and subsequently, COVID-19. Chinese scientists sequenced the genome of SARS-CoV-2 and made the data available to researchers worldwide. The SARS-CoV-2 spike protein was so effective at binding to human cells that the scientists concluded it was the result of natural selection and not the product of genetic engineering. The resulting genomic sequence data has shown that Chinese authorities rapidly detected the epidemic and that the number of COVID-19 cases have been increasing because of human-to-human transmission after a single introduction into the human population.[78]

Today, the impact of COVID-19 portends equal or more disastrous effects than the Spanish Flu of 1918–1919, the Asian Flu of 1957–1958, the Hong Kong Flu of 2003, and the severe acute respiratory syndrome (SARS-CoV-1 coronavirus) of 2003. SARS-CoV-2 novel coronavirus is a far more contagious member of the coronaviruses (CoVs), the large family of enveloped, positive-strand RNA viruses responsible for a substantial portion of upper respiratory tract infections. Many countries (e.g., China, Singapore, Hong Kong, South Korea, Italy, Spain, and the USA) have relied on an extrapolation of classic infection-control and public-health measures similar to those used for SARS-CoV-1 to contain the COVID-19 pandemic. They range from extreme quarantine measures, "shelter-in-place," "social distancing," to painstaking detailed contact tracing with hundreds of contact tracers. However, these measures may not be effective in the coming years for tackling the scale of COVID-19. Vertically integrated digital and AI technologies are being introduced for monitoring, surveillance, detection, prevention of COVID-19, and to mitigate its spread and its direct and indirect impact to worldwide health care systems.[79]

The initial reaction in many countries to COVID-19 is for health care facilities to reduce or even cease many clinical services, including closure of clinics and postponement of medical appointments or elective surgeries. However, such strategies cannot be sustained indefinitely if the COVID-19 pandemic extends beyond six months. Health care systems should plan to use digital technology 'virtual clinics' using of telehealth consultations with imaging data uploaded from peripheral sites and interpreted remotely. This would ensure that patients continue to receive standard clinical care while reducing physical crowding of patients into hospitals. Chatbots staffed by health professionals can also provide early diagnoses as well as patient education. And blockchain technologies can coordinate hospital, clinics, and pharmacy patient information.[80]

Undoubtedly, by the time you read this book, the AI literature and more so, AI programs and research in the epidemiology, public health considerations, clinical aspects, and immunological considerations regarding COVID-19 will have proliferated into a major body of new science and "disruptive technologies."[81] Indeed, the re-emergence of yet another more virulent SARS-CoV virus and global pandemic emphasize the ongoing and permanent challenge that infectious diseases pose and the need for global cooperation, AI and preparedness, even during "interim" periods.

Besides classic public-health measures for tackling the COVID-19 pandemic, in 2020, a wide range of digital technologies are being implemented that can augment and enhance these public-health strategies. This COVID-19 health care crisis of 2020 provides a distinct opportunity to enhance the applications of AI technologies for immunology in the public health domain.

REVIEW OF AI FOR EPIDEMIOLOGY AND PUBLIC HEALTH CONSIDERATIONS

1   IoTs (See Section "Internet of Things (IoT)", Chapter 1, page 5) are providing a platform that allows public-health agencies access to data for monitoring the COVID-19 pandemic. For example, the

'Worldometer'[82] provides a real-time update on the actual number of people known to have COVID-19 worldwide, including daily new cases of the disease, disease distribution by countries and severity of disease (recovered, critical condition, or death). Johns Hopkins University's Center for Systems Science and Engineering has also developed a real-time tracking map for following cases of COVID-19 across the world, using the data collected from US Centers for Disease Control and Prevention (CDC), the World Health Organization (WHO), the European Center for Disease Prevention and Control, the Chinese Center for Disease Control and Prevention (China CDC), and the Chinese website DXY.[83]

2   Big data is providing opportunities for performing modeling studies of viral activity and for guiding individual country health care policymakers to enhance preparation for the outbreak. Using three global databases, WHO International Health Regulations, the State Parties Self-Assessment Annual Reporting Tool, Joint External Evaluation reports and the Infectious Disease Vulnerability Index, health authorities are performing AI modeling studies of 'now-casting' and forecasting COVID-19 disease activity throughout the world for public-health planning and control worldwide.[84]

3   Digital technology is enhancing public-health education and communication. The government of Singapore has partnered with WhatsApp (owned by Facebook) to allow the public to receive accurate information about COVID-19 and government initiative. Multiple social-media platforms (e.g., Facebook and Twitter) are currently being used by health care agencies to provide 'real-time' updates and clarify uncertainties with the public. Also, some facial-recognition companies (e.g., SenseTime and Sunell) have adopted the GPU thermal imaging-enabled facial recognition to identify people with an elevated temperature.[85]

4   When the COVID-19 pandemic enters dangerous new phases, the critical question becomes whether and when to take aggressive public health interventions to slow down the spread of COVID-19. A study was undertaken to develop AI inspired methods for real-time forecasting and evaluating intervention strategies to curb

worldwide spread. A modified autoencoder for modeling the transmission dynamics of the epidemics is being developed and applied to the surveillance data of cumulative and new COVID-19 cases and deaths from WHO, as of March 16, 2020. Total peak number of cumulative cases and new cases in the world with later intervention could reach 255,392,154 by January 2021. However, the total peak number of cumulative cases in the world with one-week earlier intervention were reduced to 1,530,276. We observed that delaying intervention for one month caused the maximum number of cumulative cases to increase 166.89 times, and the number of deaths increase from 53,560 to 8,938,725. Disastrous consequences result if immediate action to intervene is not taken.[86]

5   MIT published a paper describing the needed changes in three areas if we want AI to be useful in future pandemics. First, prediction through database companies using a range of natural-language processing (NLP) algorithms to monitor news outlets and official health-care reports in different languages around the world; second, machine-learning models with large datasets for examining medical images to catch early signs of disease that human doctors miss, from eye disease to heart conditions to cancer; third, identifying cures through big data analysis of drug trials and design algorithms to highlight biological and molecular structures matching drugs with candidates.[87]

I began this chapter in the Incidence and Prevalence by reporting on the number of worldwide COVID-19 recorded cases and deaths to date. The number reminds me of a sad saying. "One death is a tragedy – 1,422,647 is a statistic." We can't let ourselves think that way. Maybe if we think of it as 1,422,647 personal tragedies (and growing), we'll realize what the world and each of us as caring individuals are truly enduring with this pandemic. How bad will it get? Unless a vaccine has been developed, approved, and delivered to the world's population by the time you read this, we will continue to face human tragedies, not statistics, of epic proportions. It is estimated that there are 1.7 million viruses residing in environmental ecosystems throughout the world. Let us all hope and pray that the applications of science, AI technologies and mostly, our personal and societal efforts meet and defeat this public health challenge of infectious disease pandemics and help humanity create a better place for all.

NOTES

1 Principles of epidemiology in public health practice. *Center for Disease Control and Prevention.* May 18, 2012.

2 Kelsey JL, Thompson WD, Evans AS. *Methods in observational epidemiology.* New York: Oxford University Press; 1986. p. 216.

3 Scheidel W. *The great leveler:Violence and the history of inequality from the stone age to the twenty-first century. Chapter 10: the Black Death.* Princeton, NJ: Princeton University Press; 2017. pp. 291–313.

4 Thucydides, history of the Peloponnesian War, Book 2, Chapter VII. pp. 89–100., *trans. Crawley R. Digireads.com publishing;* 2017.

5 Sabbatani S, Fiorino S. The antonine plague and the decline of the Roman empire. *Infez Med.* December 2009;17(4):261–275.

6 Horgan J. Justinian's plague (541–542 CE). *Ancient History Encyclopedia.* December 26, 2014.

7 DeWitte SN. Mortality risk and survival in the aftermath of the medieval Black Death. *PLoS one.* 2014;9(5):e96513.

8 Polio elimination in the United States. *Center for Disease Control and Prevention.* October 25, 2019.

9 Keet E. Number of reported polio cases in first months of 2019 up from 2018. *ContagionLive.* June 7, 2019.

10 Weatherspoon D. The most dangerous epidemics in U.S. history. *Healthline.* September 29, 2016.

11 Trifonov V, Khiabanian H, Rabadan R. Geographic dependence, surveillance, and origins of the 2009 influenza A (H1N1) virus. *N Engl J Med.* 2009;361(2):115–119.

12 Past pandemics. *World Health Organization.* 2020.

13 WHO: R&D Blueprint, list of Blueprint priority diseases. https://www. who.int/blueprint/priority-diseases/en/. Accessed October 2018.

14 World Health Organization (WHO). Summary of probable SARS cases with onset of illness from November 1, 2002 to July 31, 2003.

15 Huremović D. Brief history of pandemics (pandemics throughout history). Psychiatry of pandemics. *Nature Public Health Emergency Collection*. May 2019;16:7–35.

16 COVID-19 coronavirus pandemic. *Worldometer*. Last updated: March 27, 2020.

17 Coronavirus COVID-19 global cases by the center for systems science and engineering (CSSE). *Johns Hopkins University*. March 27, 2020.

18 Cui J, Li F, Shi ZL. Origin and evolution of pathogenic coronaviruses. *Nat Rev Microbiol*. 2019;17(3):181–192.

19 Wang SF, Chen KH, Chen M, et al. Human-leukocyte antigen class I Cw 1502 and class II DR 0301 genotypes are associated with resistance to severe acute respiratory syndrome (SARS) infection. *Viral Immunol*. 2011;24(5):421–426.

20 Long Q, Liu B, Deng H, et al. Antibody responses to SARS-CoV-2 in patients with COVID-19. *Nat Med*. 2020;26:845–848. doi: 10.1038/s41591-020-0897-1.

21 Zhao J, Zhao J, Mangalam AK, et al. Airway memory CD4(+) T cells mediate protective immunity against emerging respiratory coronaviruses. *Immunity*. 2016;44(6):1379–1391.

22 Woodward Davis AS, Roozen HN, Dufort MJ, et al. The human tissue-resident CCR5(+) T cell compartment maintains protective and functional properties during inflammation. *Sci Transl Med*. 2019;11(521).

23 Fan Wu F, Zhao S, Yu B, et al. A new coronavirus associated with human respiratory disease in China. *Nature*. February 3, 2020;579:265–269.

24 Terry M. Vir biotech IDs two antibodies that could be effective in preventing and treating COVID-19. *BioSpace*. March 25, 2020.

25 Collins F. Genomic study points to natural origin of COVID-19. *NIH Director's Blog*. March 26, 2020.

26 Dolan L. 8 big cats have tested positive for coronavirus at the Bronx Zoo. *CNN*. April 23, 2020.

27 Zhou P, Yang X-L, Wang X-G, et al. A pneumonia outbreak associated with a new coronavirus of probable bat origin. *Nature*. 2020;14:270–273.

28 Cao Y, Li L, Feng Z, et al. Comparative genetic analysis of the novel coronavirus (2019-nCoV/SARS-137 CoV-2) receptor ACE2 in different populations. *Cell Discov*. 2020;6:1–4.

29 Richardson P, Griffin I, Tucker C, et al. Baricitinib as potential treatment for 2019-nCoV acute respiratory disease. *Lancet*. 2020;395(10223): e30–e31.

30 Wu J. How artificial intelligence can help fight coronavirus. *Forbes Cognitive World*. March 19, 2020.

31 Zhang L, Wang DC, Huang Q. Significance of clinical phenomes of patients with COVID-19 infection: A learning from 3795 patients in 80 reports. *Clin Transl Med*. April 4, 2020. doi: 10.1002/ctm2.17.

32 Ong E, Wong MU, Huffman A, He Y. COVID-19 coronavirus vaccine design using reverse vaccinology and machine learning. Preprint. *bioRxiv*. March 21, 2020. doi: 10.1101/2020.03.20.000141.

33 Chen J, Li K, Zhang Z, et al. A survey on applications of artificial intelligence in fighting against COVID-19. *arXiv*. 2007.02202. July 4, 2020.

34 Alimadadi A, Aryal S, Manandhar I, et al. Artificial intelligence and machine learning to fight COVID-19. *Journal/Physiolgenomics*. April 3, 2020. doi.org/10.1152/physiolgenomics.00029.2020.

35 Glück T. Association of comorbidities with COVID-19 outcomes. *NEJM Journal Watch*. April 1, 2020.

36 Kass DA. COVID-19 and severe obesity: A big problem? *Ann Intern Med*. Published online August 12, 2020. doi: 10.7326/M20-5677.

37 Huang, C, et al. Clinical features of patients infected with 2019 novel coronavirus in Wuhan, China. *Lancet*. 2020;395:497–506.

38 Fox SE, Li G, Akmatbekov A, et al. Unexpected features of cardiac pathology in COVID-19 infection. *Circulation*. July 21, 2020. doi: 10.1161/Circulation aha.120.049465.

39 Liu B, Li, M, Zhou Z, et al. Can we use interleukin-6 (IL-6) blockade for coronavirus disease 2019 (COVID-19)-induced cytokine release syndrome (CRS)? *J Autoimmun*. April 10, 2020. doi: 10.1016/j.jaut.2020.102452.

40 Zhang L, Wang DC, Huang Q. Significance of clinical phenomes of patients with COVID-19 infection: A learning from 3795 patients in 80 reports. *Clin Transl Med*. April 4, 2020. doi: 10.1002/ctm2.17.

41 Service RF. Coronavirus antigen tests: Quick and cheap, but too often wrong? *Science*. May 22, 2020.

42 Marshall WF. How do COVID-19 antibody tests differ from diagnostic tests? *Mayo Clinic*. May 20, 2020.

43 Coronavirus Disease 2019. Test for past infection. *National Center for Immunization and Respiratory Diseases (NCIRD), Division of Viral Diseases*. June 30, 2020.

44 CDC Media Statement. Updated isolation guidance does not imply immunity to COVID-19. Content source: *Centers for Disease Control and Prevention*. August 14, 2020.

45 BioFire. *The BioFire FilmArray Respiratory EZ (RP EZ) Panel.* https://www. biofiredx.com/products/the-filmarray-panels/filmarray-respiratory-panel-ez/. Accessed January 17, 2020.

46 Coronaviruses: SARS, MERS, and 2019-nCoV. *Johns Hopkins Bloomberg School of Public Health.* January 21, 2020.

47 Ibid. Coronaviruses. 46.

48 D'Souza G, Dowdy D. What is herd immunity and how can we achieve it with COVID-19? *Johns Hopkins Bloomberg School of Public Health.* April 10, 2020.

49 Bergstrom CT, Dean N. What the proponents of 'natural' herd immunity don't say try to reach it without a vaccine, and millions will die. *New York Times.* May 1, 2020.

50 Ibid. Bergstrom. 49.

51 Ledford H. Antibody therapies could be a bridge to a coronavirus vaccine — but will the world benefit? *Nature.* August 12, 2020.

52 Rajewsky K. The advent and rise of monoclonal antibodies. *Nature.* November 4, 2019.

53 Guarner J, Roback JD, et al. Convalescent plasma to treat COVID-19 possibilities and challenges. *JAMA.* March 27, 2020. doi:10.1001/jama.2020.4940.

54 Brouwer PJM, Caniels TG, van der Straten K, et al. Potent neutralizing antibodies from COVID-19 patients define multiple targets of vulnerability. *Science.* August 7, 2020;369(6504):643–650. doi: 10.1126/science. abc5902.

55 Cavalcanti AB, Zampieri FG, Rosa RG, et al. Hydroxychloroquine with or without azithromycin in mild-to-moderate Covid-19. *NEJM.* July 23, 2020. doi: 10.1056/NEJMoa2019014.

56 Gautretab P, Lagierac JC, Parola P, et al. Hydroxychloroquine and azithromycin as a treatment of COVID-19: Results of an open-label non-randomized clinical trial. *Int. J. Antimicrob. Agents.* March 20, 2020;56(1):105949.

57 Beigel JH, Tomashek KM, Dodd LE, et al. Remdesivir for the treatment of Covid-19 — preliminary report. May 22, 2020. doi: 10.1056/ NEJMoa2007764.

58 Arabi YM, Mandourah Y, Al-Hameed F, et al. Corticosteroid therapy for critically ill patients with Middle East respiratory syndrome. *Am J Respir Crit Care Med.* 2018;197:757–767.

59 The Recovery Collaborative Group. Dexamethasone in hospitalized patients with Covid-19 — preliminary report. *NEJM.* July 17, 2020. doi: 10.1056/ NEJMoa2021436.

60 Prescott HC, Rice TW. Corticosteroids in COVID-19 ARDS: Evidence and hope during the pandemic. *JAMA*. Published online September 2, 2020. doi:10.1001/jama.2020.16747.

61 Anderson D, Fu D, Maquat L. COVID-19: What's RNA research got to do with it? *Univ. of Rochester NewsCenter*. April 28, 2020.

62 The vaccine testing process. *New York Times*. August 17, 2020.

63 Feng L, Wang Q, Shan C, et al. An adenovirus-vectored COVID-19 vaccine confers protection from SARS-COV-2 challenge in rhesus macaques. *Nat Commun*. 2020;11:4207. doi: 10.1038/s41467-020-18077-5.

64 Callaway E. The race for coronavirus vaccines: A graphical guide. *Nature*. April 28, 2020.

65 Gonatopoulos-Pournatzis T, Aregger M, Brown KR, et al. Genetic interaction mapping and exon-resolution functional genomics with a hybrid Cas9–Cas12a platform. *Nat. Biotechnol*. March 16, 2020; 38(5):638–648. doi: 10.1038/s41587-020-0437-z.

66 Etzioni O, DeCario N. AI can help scientists find a Covid-19 vaccine. *Wired*. March 20, 2020.

67 Collins F. Structural biology points way to coronavirus vaccine. *NIH Director's Blog*. March 3, 2020.

68 Bahrami AA, Payandeh Z, Khalili S, et al. Immunoinformatics: In Silico approaches and computational design of a multi-epitope, immunogenic protein. *Int Rev Immunol*. 2019;38(6):307–322. doi:10.1080/08830185.2019.1657426.

69 Oli AN, Obialor WO, Ifeanyichukwu MO, et al. Immunoinformatics and vaccine development: An overview. *Immunotargets Ther*. February 2020;26(9): 13–30. doi: 10.2147/ITT.S241064. PMID: 32161726.

70 Senior A, Jumper J, Hassabis D, et al. AlphaFold: Using AI for scientific discovery. *arXiv.org*>cs>arXiv:2003.11336v1. March 25, 2020.

71 Jumper J, Tunyasuvunakool K, Kohli P, Hassabis D, Team A. Computational predictions of protein structures associated with COVID-19. *arXiv.org*>cs>arXiv:2003.11336v1. March 2020.

72 Bahrami AA, Payandeh Z, Khalili S, et al. Immunoinformatics: In Silico approaches and computational design of a multi-epitope, immunogenic protein. *Int Rev Immunol*. 2019;38(6):307–322.

73 Mei X, Lee H, Diao K, et al. Artificial intelligence–enabled rapid diagnosis of patients with COVID-19. *Nat Med*. 2020;26:1224–1228. doi: 10.1038/s41591-020-0931-3.

74 Scudellari M. Five companies using AI to fight coronavirus. IEEE *Spectrum*. March 19, 2020.

75 Waleed A, Preety S, Gupta BG. Review on machine and deep learning models for the detection and prediction of Coronavirus. J. *matpr*. June 23, 2020. doi: 10.1016/j.matpr.2020.06.245.

76 Maghdid HS, Ghafoor KZ, Sadiq AS, et al. A novel AI-enabled framework to diagnose coronavirus COVID 19 using smartphone embedded sensors. *Design Study. arXiv.org > cs > arXiv*:2003.07434. May 30, 2020.

77 Ting DSW, Carin L, Dzau V, et al. Digital technology and COVID-19. *Nat Med*. March 27, 2020. doi: 10.1038/s41591-020-0824-5.

78 Scripps Research Institute. COVID-19 coronavirus epidemic has a natural origin. *ScienceDaily*. March 17, 2020.

79 Ting DSW, Carin L, Dzau V, et al. Digital technology and COVID-19. *Nat Med*. March 27, 2020. doi: 10.1038/s41591-020-0824-5.

80 Ibid. Ting. 78.

81 McIntosh K, Hirsch MS, Bloom A. Coronavirus disease 2019 (COVID-19): Epidemiology, virology, and prevention. *UpToDate.WoltersKluwer*. Topic 126981 Version 108.0. August 27, 2020.

82 https://www.worldometers.info/coronavirus/.

83 https://gisanddata.maps.arcgis.com/apps/opsdashboard/ index.html#/ bda7594740fd40299423467b48e9ecf6).

84 Joseph T, Wu JT, Leung K, Leung GM. Nowcasting and forecasting the potential domestic and international spread of the 2019-nCoV outbreak originating in Wuhan, China: a modelling study. *Lancet*. February 29, 2020;395(10225):689–697.

85 Ibid. Ting. 174.

86 Zixin H, Qiyang G, Shudi L, et al. Forecasting and evaluating intervention of Covid-19 in the *World*. arXiv:2003.09800[q-bio.PE]. March 22, 2020.

87 Heaven WD. AI could help with the next pandemic—but not with this one. MIT *Technology Review*. March 12, 2020.

88 Jamshidi MB, Lalbakhsh A, Talla J, et al. Artificial intelligence and COVID-19: Deep learning approaches for diagnosis and treatment. IEEE. June 12, 2020;8:109581–109595.

89 Naveed A., Rahman SU, Arshad MI, et al. Recapitulation of the anti-Idiotype antibodies as vaccine candidate. *Transl Med Commun* 3, 1, March 1, 2018. https://doi.org/10.1186/s41231-018-0021-4.

90 Scudellari M. Five companies using AI to fight coronavirus. IEEE *Spectrum*. March 19, 2020.

6

EMERGING TRENDS AND FUTURE DIRECTIONS FOR AI IN IMMUNOLOGY

THE INFLUENCE OF AI AND IMMUNOLOGY ON OUR PERSONAL HEALTH AND WELLNESS

In the past five chapters, we've taken, what I referred to in the Preface of this book as a deep dive into a set of rather complex subjects. We looked at innate immunology as a basic bioscience of life and what we consider "our best friend." Then we looked at its evolution from a powerful defense mechanism in our body to a potentially devastating, chronic negative force or, "our worst enemy." We tried to understand the unknown reasons why our immune system would turn on itself and interpret self as a non-self (as a foreign antigen) to produce an array of autoimmune diseases. And finally, we addressed COVID-19. It's unlikely that a day goes by that we don't read something, talk with someone, or just give thought to COVID-19. After reading this book, I would think that any of those occurrences will resurrect something you will remember from the immunology information we covered. Indeed, without an understanding of immunology and immunogenics, there can't be a full understanding of COVID-19.

As AI applies its powerful diagnostic, therapeutic, and analytical tools more and more to the bioscience of immunology and immunogenics, we will reach new levels of health and wellness. And after all is said and done, our educational journey through immunology, its demons and its better angels, will lead us to a greater understanding of what makes us healthy…or not, and how we can care for ourselves, our loved ones, and all humanity.

THE INFLUENCE OF AI AND IMMUNOLOGY ON THE PUBLIC HEALTH

The Harvard T.H. Chan School of Public Health and the Human Vaccines Project announced the Human Immunomics Initiative (HII), a joint project that aims to revolutionize the understanding of the human immune system and accelerate the creation of effective vaccines, diagnostics, and treatments. HII will specifically focus on determining the principles of effective immunity in aging populations, the world's largest growing demographic that has an immense disease burden and high morbidity and mortality in the current COVID-19 pandemic.[1]

Evolving AI concepts in public health include big data analytics, precision medicine, population health, and all the programs directed at preventive health, all having a strong immunologic component. AI algorithms are being used to create synthetic patient populations with the properties of actual patient cohorts, build personalized predictive models of drug combinations, and unraveling complex relationships between diet, microbiome, and genetics to determine comparative treatment responses.[2] Applying AI methods in immunology to accelerate the path to cures for complex human diseases are aligning with the Precision Medicine Initiative and the "All of Us" project which gives researchers and medical practitioners tools to cure people. But it also empowers individuals to monitor and take a more active role in their own health.[3]

CURRENT AND INTERMEDIATE CONSIDERATIONS OF AI APPLICATIONS FOR IMMUNOLOGY

The amount of literature, research, and data being produced relative to the field of immunology and its related sciences like immunogenics, immunotherapies, molecular biology, and on and on, are daunting. No single human source can comprehensively and competently study and derive the full breadth of such data, no less the hidden interrelationships in the data that have the greatest potential for new knowledge. Not until AI's big data analytics, capable of billions of evaluations and cross-referencing of databases in fractions of seconds, were humans able to capture the intricacies of immunology and its related sciences.

Take for example the ability we now have, thanks to health care (data) analytics to assess the trillions of variables associated with the human genome, its relationships to the immune system (immunogenomics) and how we can manipulate those relationships through procedures (immunomodulation) and pharmacodynamic interventions (immunotherapies) to treat and even prevent certain diseases (hereditary anomalies, cancers, autoimmune diseases, etc.). Such abilities have led to new medical concepts like "precision medicine," a novel approach that takes into account individual variability in genes, environment, and lifestyle for each individual person. It brings the promise of "the right treatment for the right person at the right time."[4] Also, the field of "immunoinformatics" (or computational immunology), the use of computational methods and resources for the understanding of immunological information[5] has come to the forefront of COVID-19 research and investigation. These are examples of the advances in health care that AI for immunology is creating.

LONG-RANGE CONSIDERATIONS OF AI APPLICATIONS FOR IMMUNOLOGY

The long-range view of AI in immunology can be "ambitious" ("AI Will Overtake Humans in Five Years" [Elon Musk]) to more conservative, but no less global views ("AI will reach human levels by around 2029" [Ray Kurzweil]). Whatever the view, the future of immunological research suggests continued expansion as it sharpens our ability to make discoveries in immunotherapies, like the biologics (e.g., monoclonal antibodies, vaccines, etc.), immunogenetics, and immunogenomics and its role in gene editing and engineering (e.g., CRISPR-Cas9, CAR-T replacement therapy) and stem cell transplantation. All such advances will lead to controlling and eventual curing cancers, diabetes, autoimmune diseases, and more.

Bill Gates has said, "The power of artificial intelligence is" …so incredible, it will change society in some very deep ways." A brilliant (and "accurate") epidemiologist, Michael Osterholm, wrote an essay in 2005 entitled "Preparing for the Next Pandemic" cautioning the world on proper preparation. Fifteen years later, in 2020 he writes "Time is running out to prepare for the next pandemic. We must act now with decisiveness and purpose. What will be the verdict in the next 15 years?"[6] A significant portion of the answer for COVID-19 and perhaps for all health care and the public health may well lie in AI and immunology.

NOTES

1 Harvard T.H. Chan School of Public Health. Human immunomics initiative will decode immune system, speed new vaccines. American Association for the Advancement of Science (AAAS). EurekAlert. News Release. April 14, 2020.

2 Dzobo K, Adotey S, Thomford NE, et al. Integrating artificial and human intelligence: A partnership for responsible innovation in biomedical engineering and medicine. OMICS. May 7, 2020;24(5). doi: 10.1089/omi.2019.0038.

3 National Institute of Health (NIH). The future of health begins with you. All of us and precison medicine initiative. U.S. Department of Health and Human Services (HHS). 2020.

4 Au R, Ritchie M, Hardy S, et al. Aging well: Using precision to drive down costs and increase health quality. Adv Geriatr Med Res. 2019;1:e190003. doi: 10.20900/agmr20190003.

5 Oli AN, Obialor WO, Ifeanyichukwu MO, et al. Immunoinformatics and vaccine development: An overview. Immunotargets Ther. 2020;26:13–30. doi: 10.2147/ITT.S241064.

6 Osterholm MT, Olshaker M. Chronicle of a pandemic foretold: Learning from the COVID-19 failure—before the next outbreak arrives. Foreign Affairs. July/August 2020.

INDEX

Printed in the United States
by Baker & Taylor Publisher Services